Praise

'*Who Will Get My Money When I Die?* is to my mind, with the benefit of thirty-five years' professional experience as a tax lawyer and the last ten years' pastoral experience as a Church of England priest, a book that adds significantly to the existing literature on the subject. The style throughout is informal, engaging and not technical. The text is not so much expounding the letter of the law (though due reference is made where needed) as being based on Stuart Ritchie's extensive experience in advising a wide range of clients, and there are lots of helpful real-life examples. It is certainly the case that far too many people in the UK (some 60% of the adult population) die intestate – that is, without a Will – and people need urgently to read and act upon this book, even if the mitigation of Inheritance Tax might not be such a concern to them (although there's much valuable material there too). The book also covers the essential process of choosing executors and how to decide what to put in a Will. I cannot recommend this excellent book highly enough.'
 — **Matthew Hutton**, retired solicitor,
 tax specialist, farmer and Anglican priest

'This wonderful book could be a case history of my family's journey with Stuart over the past thirty years. I was running a medium-sized company when

Stuart was recommended as someone who could advise me on business and family tax planning. He has guided me through all the areas covered in this book, as I made the journey through the sale of my business interests, all aspects of our Estate planning, including trusts, Inheritance Tax and Wills, and the optimal financial provision for my wife and two children. The result, to paraphrase a sentiment in his book, is that I can look forward to my later years secure in the knowledge that everything has been done to ensure I can have a "good death" from a financial point of view. In addition to his very high level of technical expertise, Stuart is patient, very empathetic, a good listener and a real pleasure to spend time with. What more could you ask for? This book is an invaluable guide for anyone seeking to properly organise their affairs.'

— **Peter Allez**, former Managing Director, Camden Graphics

'This is a comprehensive, user-friendly book, which provides much needed clarity to the questions an individual might ask when putting their affairs in order. Stuart Ritchie seeks to inform and educate, helping to ensure that the reader understands the issues they face, and is comfortable with how they can effectively direct their assets and enable their legacy to continue. Stuart uses his great experience to give the reader background on the practicalities, what needs to be thought about and discussed, and whether the decisions made are likely to achieve the

desired outcomes. I highly recommend the book to laymen and professional practitioners alike.'
— **Russell Bussey**, IMC, Owner and Director, Bussey Consulting

'*Who Will Get My Money When I Die?* was not a book I expected to hold my attention for long. However, the engaging style in which Stuart writes, illustrating the complex subject of Inheritance Tax with some excellent real-life examples, made me stop and consider how well have I planned for the impact of Inheritance Tax on my Estate and how it will affect my children. If you have any doubts or concerns about Inheritance Tax and its possible impact on you, this is an invaluable read.'
— **Robert Forster**, Management Consultant and former General Manager, Nikon Corporation

'In *Who Will Get My Money When I Die?*, Stuart provides clear and concise guidance on the ins and outs of Inheritance Tax and related issues. The book is written in plain English and avoids jargon, making it accessible to a wide range of readers. Stuart begins by explaining the basics of when and how to start preparing Wills and probate, before delving into more complex topics, such as life assurance, and a list of special circumstances that we should be aware of. Stuart also provides helpful pointers on a variety of other subjects related to inheritance, such as how to talk to your family about your wishes, how to choose an executor and how to deal with the emotional aspects of inheritance. Stuart does a good job of explaining complex concepts in a way that is easy to understand, making the book informative and helpful. Overall, *Who Will Get My Money When I Die?* is a valuable resource for anyone who wants to make sure their assets are distributed according to their wishes.'

— **Gordon Gilchrist**, Marketing Director, 2020 Innovation Group

WHO WILL GET MY MONEY WHEN I DIE?

THE CONCISE GUIDE TO MAKING
YOUR WILL AND REDUCING
THE IMPACT OF INHERITANCE
TAX ON YOUR ESTATE

STUART RITCHIE FCA CTA

Rethink

First published in Great Britain in 2024 by
Rethink Press (www.rethinkpress.com)

© Copyright Stuart Ritchie

All rights reserved. No part of this publication may be reproduced, stored in or introduced into a retrieval system, or transmitted, in any form, or by any means (electronic, mechanical, photocopying, recording or otherwise) without the prior written permission of the publisher.

The right of Stuart Ritchie to be identified as the author of this work has been asserted by him in accordance with the Copyright, Designs and Patents Act 1988.

This book is sold subject to the condition that it shall not, by way of trade or otherwise, be lent, resold, hired out, or otherwise circulated without the publisher's prior consent in any form of binding or cover other than that in which it is published and without a similar condition including this condition being imposed on the subsequent purchaser.

Contents

Foreword   1

Introduction   3

PART ONE   Setting The Scene   9

1 **Death – An Inconvenient Truth**   13
     When and how to start preparing   13
     The legacy we leave behind   15
     The significance of life expectancy   17
     Is there such a thing as a good death?   21

2 **Wills And Probate**   25
     Do you even need a Will?   26
     What makes a good Will?   35
     Appointing guardians   38
     What a good executor looks like   43

3	**What Do I Own?**	**47**
	Financial structures	49
	Trusts and settlements	51
	The main types of asset classes	52
	Trophy assets	55
	Overview	60
4	**Succession Planning For Your Business**	**61**
	Who should inherit your business and when?	62
	The importance of meticulous planning	66
	How far in advance to start planning to pass the business on	69
	What if your preferred nominated successor isn't ready to take control?	71

PART TWO   The Fundamentals Of IHT Planning   73

5	**Avoiding The Bear Traps Set By HMRC To Defeat Your IHT Planning**	**77**
	Gifts with reservation of benefit – the GWROB rules	78
	Why caution is needed	80
	The general anti-abuse rule (GAAR)	84
	Debts not repaid after death	85
	Agricultural property or business property relief	86

Challenges to whether your IHT planning has been properly implemented	86
The 'great escape' from HMRC by paying full consideration	90
The risk factor of IHT injustices	91
The last laugh?	92

6 Assets On Which No IHT Is Due — **95**

Agricultural property relief	98
Business property relief	104
Pensions	108
Gifts between husband and wife and civil partners	110

7 The Impact Of Life Assurance — **113**

The benefits of life assurance	114
Understanding your choices	117
Risks	119
Planning to avoid failure	121

8 Making Lifetime Gifts And Surviving Seven Years — **123**

Gifts that are exempt from IHT	126
Potentially exempt transfers (PETs) for IHT	132

Gifts chargeable to IHT at the lifetime tax rate	134
To gift or not to gift?	135

9 Putting Assets Into Trust For Future Generations — 139

The great advantage of discretionary trusts	142
Different types of trusts and settlements	144
How IHT applies under the 6% regime	148
Trusts not in the 6% regime	150

PART THREE Bring It All Together — 153

10 The Four Building Blocks Of Estate Planning — 155

Building block 1: Assessing your personal wealth	157
Building block 2: Lifetime giving	159
Building block 3: Structuring your Will	160
Building block 4: Death benefits	165

11 Special Circumstances — 167

1. Blended families	168
2. Orphaned children	170
3. Young adults	172
4. International dimension	174
5. Persons with a disability	179

6. Mental incapacity	180
7. Unmarried parents	181
8. Two-year rule 'let-out'	182

12 The Peace Of Mind Of Having An Estate Plan — **185**

Benefits of an Estate plan — 185

13 How A Letter Of Wishes Strengthens Your Estate Plan — **191**

Conclusion — **195**

Acknowledgements — **199**

The Author — **201**

Foreword

We have in this country, at this point in our social history, an uncomfortable relationship with the subject of death. There is a reticence to deal head on with what is (along with taxes) one of the inescapable certainties of life itself.

By asking the simple question, 'Who will get my money when I die?', Stuart Ritchie tackles with direct pragmatism the inconvenient truth of our own deaths and the real-world consequences for our loved ones of ignoring its inevitability.

Equipped with a better understanding of the legal, financial and fiscal framework in which our deaths take place, positive action can be taken to avoid pitfalls and, in some circumstances, influence for the better the future of our heirs. This is precisely what this book aims to do. By taking the reader through each of the relevant topics, without jargon and with examples, this book unpacks even the most technical aspect of passing on an Estate and puts it in a context that is readily understood.

This is the book advisors in this area will want their clients to read. It is a much less daunting exercise on both sides to assist a well-informed client to put their plans into action when they have been expertly guided in their thinking about the deceptively simple question of who will receive their money when they die.

Laura Dadswell
Tax and trust planning solicitor
Partner, Penningtons Manches Cooper LLP
Member of the Society of Trust and Estate Practitioners (STEP)

Introduction

It constantly staggers me that a large proportion of the UK population never get around to making their Will and thus die intestate, meaning all assets will be distributed according to intestacy law. According to research published in March 2023 by Unbiased, more than 31 million adults – nearly 60% of adults in the UK – haven't made a Will.[1] For some, that is a deliberate choice due to the perceived benefits of not making a Will, although these are limited. For many, however, it's more about people sticking their heads in the sand and hoping they can avoid the inevitable. The relief people show once they commit to arranging their Wills tells me that what I offer is not only valuable, it also

---

1   N Green, 'What if I have no will? The problem of intestacy' (Unbiased, 2023), www.unbiased.co.uk/discover/personal-finance/family/what-if-i-have-no-will, accessed 17 March 2023

allows them to enjoy the rest of their lives to the fullest extent possible. This book is intended for anyone who either has, or believes they may have, an Inheritance Tax (IHT) liability. It's also written for those concerned about ensuring that their wishes as to who inherits their money when they die are properly fulfilled.

I am a fellow of the Institute of Chartered Accountants in England and Wales and a member of the Chartered Institute of Taxation. I am also chair of the Private Client Committee of the Tax Faculty of the Institute of Chartered Accountants in England and Wales (ICEAW). This position not only extends my influence within the profession as a whole; it also places me at the heart of the dialogue between the small group of leading accountants that operate in private client taxation. The resultant conversations offer me unique insights into developments and trends within the world of high-net-worth and ultra-high-net-worth individuals. This is a natural extension of the areas I have specialised in for over thirty years – from private client taxation issues, which includes inheritance and succession planning, to helping to agree complex taxation issues for clients (both on- and offshore) with His Majesty's Revenue and Customs (HMRC).

At the start of my accountancy career, I trained and studied while working for two of the leading private client accountancy firms in London, leading me to join Rawlinson & Hunter, one of the top four private client accountancy firms in London.

INTRODUCTION

Once a qualified chartered accountant and chartered tax advisor, I began working in private client taxation, as well as being exposed to IHT and the giving of succession advice. In many respects, this was a 'baptism of fire' – some of the tax returns I worked on were associated with clients of the highest profile and comprised huge volumes of data with complex, high-value entries. These required intense and scrupulous attention to detail, marking the beginning of my specialist interest in working within the private client sector.

After six years with Rawlinson & Hunter, I was hired as a manager at the relatively small private client practice, Dixon Wilson. In 1996, in recognition of my high work rate and technical ability as well as my skill in attracting new clients, I was invited to become a partner.

In 2003 I decided once more to consider my future prospects and founded my own accountancy firm, Ritchie Phillips LLP. From its inception, I clearly articulated that the firm's scope was to provide specialist taxation and accountancy services in the following four key areas:

1. **High-net-worth and ultra-high-net-worth individuals:** Typically (but not exclusively), these are high achievers and influencers who hold property interests, investment portfolios with equities, bonds, and investment funds;

together with high levels of cash deposits and borrowings. My aim is to help these individuals come to enjoy the benefits that such wealth affords, without the burdens.

2. **Entrepreneurs with growing businesses:** Bringing together the personal and business interests of an entrepreneur, typically with a fast-growth business, I help create structures that work for both the continued growth of the business and its potential sale. The issues that typically arise include:

   - How the subsequent wealth should be distributed within a family – whether it should be centred on one individual; or whether other family members, or trusts and charities, should receive a share of that wealth

   - How the tax liability of that distribution can be mitigated

3. **Resident foreigners and non-UK domiciliaries:** I advise both UK and non-UK residents in respect of the Statutory Residence Test and how to remain non-UK tax resident while visiting the UK for some of each year, either for social or business purposes. I am also experienced in the UK special tax system known as the remittance basis, which applies to individuals not domiciled in the UK (non-doms) and who are eligible to claim this basis.

4. **Individuals or businesses subject to HMRC tax investigation or dispute:** Representing individuals and businesses under investigation for alleged tax irregularities is an important part of my work, as these circumstances can place a significant strain on a client and their personal and business relationships. Understanding the HMRC approach and objectives is key to settling any such investigation, and I ensure that the scope of the enquiry is both clear and contained.

Before I offer advice to anyone seeking my help, my principal job is to listen. I'm always curious about how people think and behave, and about what is important for them. In relation to Estate planning, simply taking that first step in thinking about their Will represents a leap forward for some, especially if they have been afraid of confronting an inconvenient truth – that one day, we will all die.

This book is not intended as a substitute for professional advice. Rather, its purpose is to inform you on some of the decisions you might make. Those decisions, however, need to be made in conjunction with an appropriately qualified and experienced professional advisor. The casual say-so of a friend comes with the dangers of incomplete advice – it certainly won't guarantee your best interests are served or solve what will happen to your money, including the impact on your loved ones, when you die.

The book is therefore written in plain English and seeks to avoid jargon that often adds to people's confusion and their resistance to engage. My aim is to move you towards a position where you feel you can take appropriate advice and follow some of the suggestions I make.

At this point, a word of caution: I will not cover areas relating to readers who are not domiciled or not resident in the UK, due to the breadth and complexity of the relevant tax rules and regulations. There are also different laws in Scotland and Northern Ireland – for example, relating to succession – which are beyond the scope of this book. Those areas rightly deserve a whole book in their own right. This book will reflect the many processes I guide my clients through to enable them to access the opportunities that will reduce their IHT liability. Reading it will enable you also to plan with confidence who will inherit your wealth, including any interest in a family business.

My experience, in seeing occasions when matters have turned sour within a family who then need my help, has fed my mission to write this book. More important, I've been able to help families discover options they didn't imagine were possible in planning for who will get their money when they die.

PART ONE
SETTING THE SCENE

In over thirty years of helping people make arrangements for their Wills, I've come to learn that often their biggest concern isn't about death per se. Rather, my clients are most concerned when they have to think about passing on their wealth. Their first question is usually about to whom they should bequeath their wealth, followed by questions about how much each beneficiary should receive.

More often than not, an individual will leave their Estate, ie their money and property (often but not always in its entirety), to their family, to non-family members or to institutions such as charities. As we begin to explore the options more fully, people also express concerns about the impact of leaving a potentially sizeable Estate to their successors, as well as how they themselves might best provide for their own future needs in old age and possibly ill health.

The ramifications of death duties, most obviously in the form of IHT liabilities, is one issue that rears its head with predictable reliability. That's not to suggest that anyone disagrees with the concept of taxation, since its core function is to provide benefits to society as a whole. It's just that people don't really know how to calculate the full potential value of their Estate in advance of their death. This can therefore remain a grey and murky area, which, if not addressed properly, can result in some unpleasant surprises and headaches for beneficiaries to muddle through in the early days of mourning. Under these circumstances, nobody wants HMRC beating down their doors demanding its legitimate share. In fact, much of the aggravation can be ameliorated ahead of the merry dance that follows.

It may surprise you when I say that, while IHT is one of the most hated of all the taxes collectable by HMRC, it is also the most 'voluntary' tax; how much your Estate pays over on your death is, more or less, entirely in your control. In fact, it's not even necessary to die to enjoy the fruits of the tax exemptions and reliefs, which this book will explain. Perhaps that's why it's surprising to learn that, since 2010, receipts from IHT have increased from £1.5 billion to more than £7.1 billion per annum.[2] This isn't because the State is a ravenous raptor that swoops down to gorge on the bounty. It's mostly due to the total asset values having increased exponentially at a rapid rate, particularly in the property sector, following the financial crash of 2008.

It could also be argued that too many people remain unaware of legitimate means by which they can limit the amount of IHT liabilities due upon their death, and also because they simply do not know the full extent of their personal wealth or know enough about the strategies available to mitigate future tax liabilities within their own lifetime. Throughout Part One, I will describe the areas you can consider looking into should you want to address this area. That, of course, requires us first to acknowledge the elephant in the room: our mortality.

---

[2] HM Revenue & Customs, 'HMRC tax receipts and National Insurance contributions for the UK (monthly bulletin)' (HMRC, 2023), www.gov.uk/government/statistics/hmrc-tax-and-nics-receipts-for-the-uk/hmrc-tax-receipts-and-national-insurance-contributions-for-the-uk-new-monthly-bulletin, accessed 29 November 2023

1
Death – An Inconvenient Truth

Without meaning to state the obvious, death inevitably marks the end of life for everyone, and there's simply no way of avoiding it. Death is an 'inconvenient truth'. Some of us will die in ways outside of our control, as a result of an accident, an unexpected event or an undiagnosed medical condition. For others, death may take its time, counting down the months and days until it finally arrives.

When and how to start preparing

Happily, many of us will be unaware of the moment of death itself. With that said, death (and dying) can be approached in a positive way; many who are approaching the end of their lives wish for nothing more than a peaceful death.

Sudden, unexpected fatalities account for anything between 10 and 20% of the total number of deaths in any one year. The statistics therefore show that it's more than likely that any one of the remaining 80 to 90% can have at least some degree of control over their death. Even if doctors have told someone they have only a limited amount of time remaining, at least that offers them the chance to put their affairs in order and to say their proper goodbyes. If nothing else, this can lead to a state of mind where an individual can be at peace with themselves, with their family and with their friends, before their life's work is finished.

I've encountered some people who allow superstition to stand in their way, such as 'Susan', who told me, 'I'm not going to make a Will, because if I do, God will know he can take me away from this world.' It could be argued that this is an irrational train of thought, but in Susan's opinion, it made complete sense. However, I'm happy to say that I've only rarely come across this way of thinking. I find that most people are keen to discover the various options in respect of their Estate planning; and that context then clarifies everything they need to arrange their Wills.

When a client knows only a short period of their life remains, our conversations can naturally be intensely emotional. Others who reasonably expect a long and normal life ahead of them may approach the matter on a more pragmatic basis. My concern with *all* clients is in learning what they want to happen to their money, if indeed they know. If they don't have any clear idea or know what options are available, including charitable bequests, we can begin to assess those options in full. In the most part, it's the start of a process that determines who will get what, and how they can navigate the potential complications that arise from their relationships with their partners – married or otherwise – and any offspring they wish to benefit from their Estate.

The legacy we leave behind

In going through this process, it often comes as a surprise to wealthy clients – those who are in the fortunate position of having more money than they need for themselves – that we enter into discussing the possibilities of lifetime giving. This is where the individual makes a gift while still alive, which then reduces their IHT liabilities upon the occasion of their death (which I discuss in more detail in Part Two).

For some individuals, this option is out of the question, either because they don't approve of lifetime giving or because they want to retain as much control as possible of their wealth during their life. I then need to make them aware of the impact, in respect of IHT liabilities, of all that money sitting in their personal Estate at the point they pass away. Only once that potential amount can be quantified can we begin a conversation about the implications of the IHT payable if matters were arranged differently.

Thinking more acutely about the sort of legacy people want to leave behind sharpens the mind – not only in financial terms but also in respect of longer-lasting memorable matters. Decisions we make at this point can help keep us alive in the memories of others. The notion of leaving a legacy speaks to the fact that it's possible for your life's work to continue after you've died.

> **CASE STUDY: The Gates legacy**
>
> An obvious example of legacy planning is Bill and Melinda Gates, who have established their own charitable foundations, into which they've transferred a significant portion of their wealth during their lifetimes.
>
> When they eventually die, it is expected an even greater portion of their wealth will be transferred to these foundations, as the Gates know their children won't need all of their remaining wealth. Instead, they have focused on worthy causes in the world, which they consider to be much more important.[3]

---

3   T Huddleston, Jr, 'Bill Gates plans to give away "virtually all" his $113 billion—here's the impact that could actually have' (CNBC, 2022), www.cnbc.com/2022/07/15/bill-gates-plans-to-give-away-virtually-all-his-113-billion-fortune.html, accessed 26 March 2023

I find it interesting that, in cases where my clients have left large legacies to their children or other relatives, the beneficiaries often don't consider that money as being their own. Instead, they tend to see themselves as trustees, and that the benefit of the money is to be passed on in much the same way as they received it.

No matter what legacy decisions are reached, few of us will have control over our final moment in life. However, in planning what will happen to our money after we die, we can mitigate to a certain degree the effect of the inconvenient truth we all face. Acknowledging and accepting this degree of control results in a huge sense of relief; the knowledge that we have carefully managed planning gives us one less thing to be anxious about. In fact, I'd go so far as saying that, instead of worrying about the inevitable, full and proper legacy planning enables you to concentrate on enjoying life to the full. This is despite the fact that actuaries can seemingly predict with uncanny accuracy when you might expect to pass away, barring any unexpected accidents.

The significance of life expectancy

An actuary bases their predictions on contributory lifestyle factors such as smoking or being overweight, which normally result in a shorter life span. The good news is that the average UK life expectancy is high – close to the early eighties for both men and women – whereas in the 1970s the expectations were nearer to seventy-five for women and seventy-two for men.[4]

While actuaries will consider all lifestyle factors, they do not play any part in the making of a Will, which is important in respect of valuing Estates. Because actuaries are mainly spot on with their predictions for average life expectancies, they also provide reliable data as to how much money pension providers need to set aside to fund pension schemes, taking into account annual inflationary increases.

Knowing the precise details of your pension scheme is vital in determining what happens to your pension when you die, dependent on the scheme itself. If you have a traditional, defined benefit pension scheme, there will be no pot of money to leave to your heirs, unless a dependant's pension provision is included. If, however, you hold a defined contribution scheme, there will be a lump sum to be paid out to a spouse, a partner or children when you die, particularly if you die younger than expected; but when that money's gone, it's gone.

The other area where actuaries become meaningfully involved relates to life insurance policies. Because these policies are designed to pay out in the event of

---

4   Office for National Statistics, 'Mortality in England and Wales: Past and projected trends in average lifespan' (ONS, 2022), www.ons.gov.uk/peoplepopulationandcommunity/birthsdeathsandmarriages/lifeexpectancies/articles/mortalityinenglandandwales/pastandprojectedtrendsinaveragelifespan, accessed 26 March 2023

your death, the life insurance company will want to know how long you're likely to live for. On arranging the policy, you will therefore be required to complete numerous questionnaires and attend medicals, the results of which are then assessed by professional experts and actuaries, who determine your predicted life expectancy. This forms the basis of your premiums and the eventual payout to your beneficiaries.

Naturally, some people live beyond actuaries' expectations, and others die before the calculated date of death. While an actuary might be a consistently reliable predictor of life expectancy, the inconvenient truth as far as they are concerned is that they cannot see the future with 100% accuracy. However, from your point of view, knowing that there could be a sum of money available to your beneficiaries upon your death emphasises the importance of controlling what happens to the life assurance proceeds.

Whether you like it or not, you shouldn't ignore the inconvenient truths surrounding your death, no matter how tempting it is to bury your head in the sand. Instead, understanding the available advice is key in extrapolating the information that's relevant to you and your wishes.

If the above has piqued your interest, you might be tempted to turn to one of the many online life-expectancy calculators. Do this by all means, but please remember that they are essentially only general indicators. They simply do not delve into the same level of detail as actuaries, so I advise approaching them with caution. I certainly wouldn't want to base any of my discussions on data derived from an online calculator, especially when considering potential IHT liabilities and lifetime giving options.

> **CASE STUDY: Too much money to spend in a lifetime**
>
> One of my clients, in his early seventies and with a spouse of a similar age, had sold his business, leaving him with a multimillion-pound wealth. He sought my advice after investing the proceeds into buy-to-let residential property schemes as well as some stocks and shares, leaving some cash to spare. He wanted to discuss the interest on the loan he'd taken in respect of his buy-to-let portfolio, but it struck me, with interest rates so low at the time, that he needn't be that concerned with income tax issues.
>
> When I asked about his family situation, he explained that he and his wife had two children, both of whom were married with families of their own, and each with a mortgage of £1 million.
>
> My direct question was why he wouldn't simply pay off his children's mortgages now. My rationale was simple: it was his and his wife's intention that their children would inherit everything when they both passed away; and, given my client's age, it was unlikely he and his wife would ever fully need to draw on their multimillion-pound wealth. I therefore asked

> if he would consider taking action during his lifetime to help his children, as hardworking as they were, by paying off their mortgages. Not only would they benefit from this act of huge generosity, but my client and his wife would also get to enjoy that moment. On a practical level, they would also reduce the IHT liabilities by the time the Estate was to be passed onto the children.
>
> My client took up my suggestion, and the positive, beneficial impact felt by all the family was immense. They could all enjoy their lives more fully in the face of the inconvenient truth.

Is there such a thing as a good death?

Who wouldn't admit to at some time wishing to live for as long as possible? While this may ring true, there are also other truisms surrounding death that are actually far more important and eminently achievable, such as wanting to lead a good life, wanting to love and be loved, and wanting to have a 'good' death.

While it is often said that death doesn't need to be feared, the process of dying often is, largely due to the absence of knowledge of when, where and how one's death will occur. That very lack of control causes the greatest concern to individuals, and much of the fear stems from us not knowing if we will have completely fulfilled our life's objectives.

The advantage of a good death – where your final wishes, including your care plan, are carried out before you die – is often seen as the concluding act of a life well lived, even if by logical extension we will be completely unaware of it.

In a study into end-of-life care, carried out by the Kaiser Family Foundation (a US-based non-profit organisation focused on health) in association with *The Economist*, it was discovered that living as long as possible was not the most important consideration. Rather, of greater importance were:

- Maintaining financial independence at end of life so as not to burden family members
- Having a good death, where one's own medical care wishes are followed
- Family members not being burdened by one's care decisions
- Being with loved ones at the point of death
- Being comfortable and without pain
- Being at peace spiritually[5]

If the same questions were posed to younger individuals, the response could be significantly

---

5 L Hamel, B Wu and M Brodie, *Views and Experiences with End-of-Life Medical Care in the U.S.* (KFF, 2017), https://files.kff.org/attachment/Report-Views-and-Experiences-with-End-of-Life-Medical-Care-in-the-US, accessed 20 March 2023

different, especially in prioritising long-life expectancy. However, as we mature, our priorities change – we all recognise (subconsciously or otherwise) that, despite our previous vigour of youth, none of us can escape the inconvenient truth. We become more interested in trying to make the best of a 'bad' situation as we focus on how we might achieve a good death. Principally, that relies on receiving the medical care desired, with us having spoken to medical practitioners while we have legal capacity. We gain comfort in knowing that our cogently expressed wishes will be carried out in full when we pass away.

In making such advance decisions in respect of your care towards the end of your life, the emotional burden can be lifted from your family and children, and possibly also your grandchildren and good friends. Those people then won't have to shoulder the heavy responsibility of making decisions on your behalf when you might be too ill to decide for yourself. They can simply be with you, as you wish, and show their love for you.

What's most important depends on the stage of life each person is at when they think about their future death. As we grow older, our outlook changes and we may not always be concerned, for example, about tax implications. My role is to listen carefully with an open mind to my clients' concerns and offer them my best advice based on their circumstances at that time, perhaps offering options they had not known were available to them. A client might initially approach me to discuss IHT planning issues, but usually something entirely different transpires. The conversation often moves on to them talking about what they want to happen to their wealth when they die and what the most important considerations are, and rarely is that exclusively about tax.

Younger couples almost always say they want all their money to be used in caring for their children, especially should they both tragically pass away when their children were still of dependent age, or if their children had any special life-long needs due to disabilities. Conversely, where the client is older and enjoys wealth in excess of what they reasonably need during their lifetime, they may think more dynastically, in seeking to create a fund that endows the family for many generations to come, sometimes also with a charitable focus.

There is simply no one-size-fits-all solution in planning for that good death. Your planning will depend on you and your circumstances, and often thinking beyond what you might consider reasonably possible. That may, or may not, be down to meeting your obvious immediate needs; it could also be about crafting succession arrangements to bestow your successors with the benefit of your wealth without the burden. The notion of a good death in the face of the inconvenient truth therefore lies in making sure that, when you pass your money on, it goes to the people you want to benefit most, with you knowing that your wishes will be carried out.

2
Wills And Probate

Probate is the entire legal and financial process for dealing with the Estate of someone who has died. When you create a Will, you can specify one or more executors – people who will be responsible for carrying out your wishes, as detailed in your Will. Your executor may be a friend or a family member, or you may choose to appoint a solicitor, a chartered accountant or some other professional advisor.

The executor needs to apply for a grant of probate – a legal document that gives them the authority to deal with the deceased's Estate. The probate process ends once all taxes and debts have been paid and the Estate distributed.

WHO WILL GET MY MONEY WHEN I DIE?

If you don't create a Will before you die, no one will have immediate authority to administer your Estate. The courts will then need to appoint an administrator to oversee the administration or your money and property.

Do you even need a Will?

The first question clients normally ask me is whether they should make a Will, to which my answer is yes – ideally, they should. The second question is whether it is necessary to make a Will to ensure that wealth is passed on to their successors, to which I am duty-bound to respond that no, it isn't. In essence, you can choose one of two ways to proceed:

1. Write a Will so that your wishes are carried out in accordance with your intentions.

2. Not write a Will, instead allowing the intestacy law of the land to determine the outcome for you.

Intestacy rules are, in principle, quite straightforward, but whether they work for you is another matter.

Intestacy law can act harshly in a number of circumstances and deliver unwanted outcomes. For example:

- **Intestacy makes no provision for unmarried or unregistered partners.** Regardless of the length of the relationship, the surviving partner will not automatically inherit anything, although they can make an Inheritance Act claim, or a '1975 Act' claim, as it is frequently known. Alternatively, the family can legally vary the distribution of the Estate to provide for the partner.

- **Intestacy does not recognise stepchildren.** Only natural and adopted children are recognised. Stepchildren may have a valid claim, or the family can legally vary the distribution within the family to provide for the stepchildren.

- **Intestacy requires children to take their inheritance at the age of eighteen.** However, most parents hold the view that children need to be much older before having control of large sums of money.

- **Intestacy will make running your own business difficult.** If you are the owner of an unincorporated business, a validly executed Will can include special executors to run the business, whereas intestacy has no such provision.

- **Intestacy may result in disputes over what are personal possessions.** These are defined as anything that is not monetary, business assets or held as an investment. Disputes often arise over what is held as investment; for example, whether the possessions will pass entirely to a new spouse, or whether they will form part of the Estate inherited by, say, the children from a first marriage.

- **Intestacy does not leave legacies to distant relatives, godchildren, friends, carers or charities.** Of course, the family can legally vary the distribution within the family to provide for others, but whatever actions they decide upon might not be in accordance with your wishes, simply because you've not made your wishes known.

- **Intestacy may not be the most tax-efficient way to distribute your Estate.** If you die intestate, your loved ones could then be landed with a hefty IHT bill from HMRC. Often, an individual's desired objectives can be achieved by carefully and tax-efficiently structuring their financial affairs, which are then stated in their Will. It goes without saying that intestacy might result in an unnecessarily increased liability to IHT.

Of course, not everyone gets around to drawing up a Will before they die, while others may not make a valid Will – there are often issues with homemade Wills.

According to research, and widely reported in the British media, nearly 60% of the UK adult population are at risk of dying intestate.[6] It might surprise you that this is a deliberate choice by some people. This is chiefly because the law surrounding intestacy is inherently simple – whenever someone dies, their

---

6 N Green, 'What if I have no will? The problem of intestacy' (Unbiased, 2023), www.unbiased.co.uk/discover/personal-finance/family/what-if-i-have-no-will, accessed 17 March 2023

wealth and possessions pass on to someone else – so people feel confident in not making a Will. Intestacy is, however, not to be recommended.

The following two diagrams show the different outcomes of what will happen to your Estate – first in the context of being married or joined in a legally recognised civil partnership; and second, when people are single, or where they cohabit, but the union is not recognised in law.

In the diagrams you will see that, if married or in a civil partnership with no children or grandchildren, if you were to die intestate, your spouse or civil partner would inherit everything. If you have children or grandchildren, your spouse or civil partner would inherit the household contents and your personal effects, plus £322,000 and half of the rest, with your children receiving the other half. Furthermore, your spouse or civil partner would be entitled to apply for letters of administration – a court-issued document that allows someone to act as Estate administrator.

If you and your spouse or civil partner jointly own any property that is held as a joint tenancy (rather than as tenants in common), your spouse or civil partner will inherit your share in the property automatically under the law for joint tenancies, regardless of you dying intestate.

The position is far more complex if you die when not married or in a civil partnership, as a cohabitee has no right to an inheritance under the rules of intestacy. It would then be necessary for the court to work through the varying degrees of relationships within your family, depending on whether they have outlived you, to determine who would inherit your Estate. It is worth noting that those who inherit also get to administer your Estate. In the worst case, if no members of your family are identified, the Crown – the State – takes everything.

In certain circumstances, the State itself is the sole beneficiary of your Estate. Interestingly, in Cornwall, if a person dies intestate, an ancient provision in the law allows the Duke of Cornwall to inherit that Estate. The previous Duke of Cornwall, now King Charles, availed himself of that practice in order to support his own charities and his bursaries at Gordonstoun, the private school in Scotland where he was educated. As extreme and rare that occurrence is, it still musters several millions of pounds each year.

The overriding point is that, when someone dies, society demands their wealth should pass to someone else. Logically, it would serve no purpose whatsoever for that wealth to remain in a state of limbo. Deciding on whom you wish to inherit your Estate (or not) is entirely up to you, thanks to the UK's unique complete freedom (compared with our European neighbours) of testamentary disposition, save for one or two statutory provisions that are quite rightly buried deep within hefty tomes and needn't concern us here.

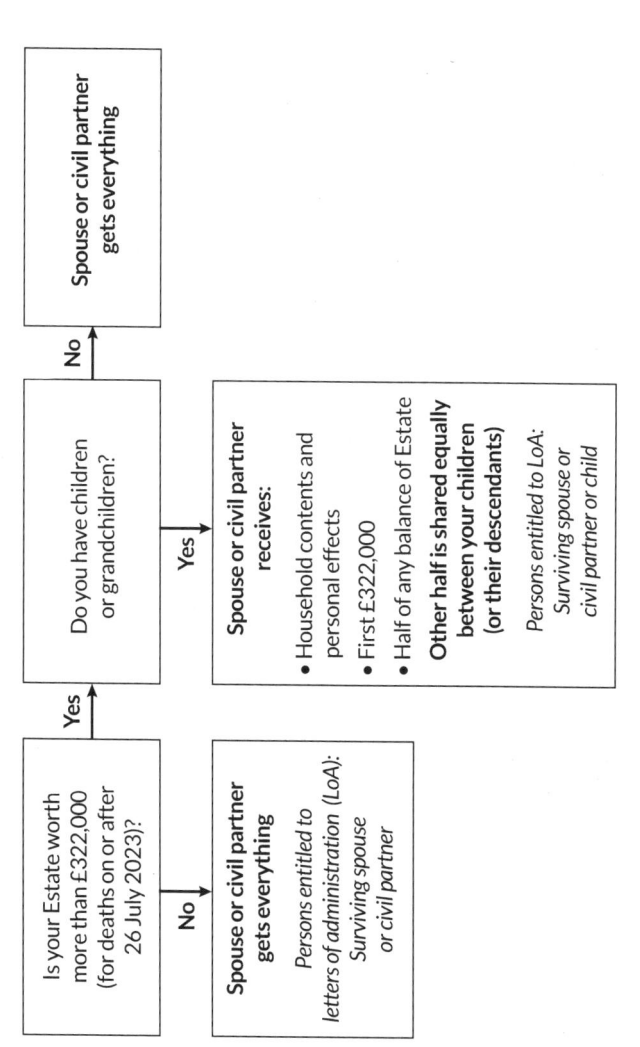

```
┌─────────────────────┐
│ Is your Estate worth│         ┌──────────────────┐   No    ┌─────────────────┐
│ more than £322,000  │── Yes ──▶│ Do you have      │────────▶│ Spouse or civil │
│ (for deaths on or   │         │ children         │         │ partner gets    │
│ after 26 July 2023)?│         │ or grandchildren?│         │ everything      │
└─────────────────────┘         └──────────────────┘         └─────────────────┘
         │                               │
         No                              Yes
         ▼                               ▼
┌──────────────────────┐        ┌────────────────────────────┐
│ Spouse or civil      │        │ Spouse or civil partner    │
│ partner gets         │        │ receives:                  │
│ everything           │        │ • Household contents and   │
│                      │        │   personal effects         │
│ Persons entitled to  │        │ • First £322,000           │
│ letters of           │        │ • Half of any balance of   │
│ administration (LoA):│        │   Estate                   │
│ Surviving spouse     │        │                            │
│ or civil partner     │        │ Other half is shared       │
└──────────────────────┘        │ equally between your       │
                                │ children (or their         │
                                │ descendants)               │
                                │                            │
                                │ Persons entitled to LoA:   │
                                │ Surviving spouse or        │
                                │ civil partner or child     │
                                └────────────────────────────┘
```

Intestacy when married or in a civil partnership

(Note: 'Children' refers to your own children, whether legitimate or illegitimate, and adopted children. It does not include stepchildren.)

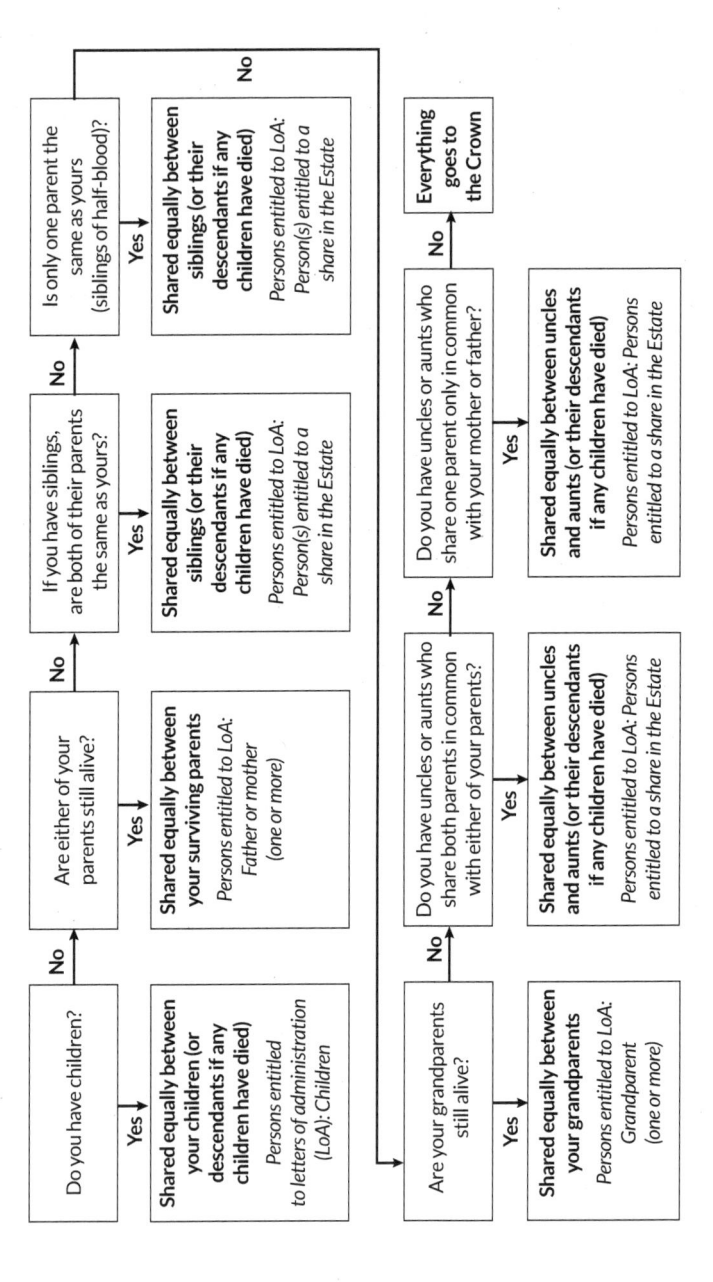

Intestacy when not married or in a civil partnership

Do you have children?

- **Yes** → Shared equally between your children (or descendants if any children have died)
  Persons entitled to letters of administration (LoA): Children

- **No** → **Are either of your parents still alive?**

  - **Yes** → Shared equally between your surviving parents
    Persons entitled to LoA: Father or mother (one or more)

  - **No** → **If you have siblings, are both of their parents the same as yours?**

    - **Yes** → Shared equally between siblings (or their descendants if any children have died)
      Persons entitled to LoA: Person(s) entitled to a share in the Estate

    - **No** → **Is only one parent the same as yours (siblings of half-blood)?**

      - **Yes** → Shared equally between siblings (or their descendants if any children have died)
        Persons entitled to LoA: Person(s) entitled to a share in the Estate

      - **No** → **Are your grandparents still alive?**

        - **Yes** → Shared equally between your grandparents
          Persons entitled to LoA: Grandparent (one or more)

        - **No** → **Do you have uncles or aunts who share both parents in common with either of your parents?**

          - **Yes** → Shared equally between uncles and aunts (or their descendants if any children have died)
            Persons entitled to LoA: Persons entitled to a share in the Estate

          - **No** → **Do you have uncles or aunts who share one parent only in common with your mother or father?**

            - **Yes** → Shared equally between uncles and aunts (or their descendants if any children have died)
              Persons entitled to LoA: Persons entitled to a share in the Estate

            - **No** → Everything goes to the Crown

WILLS AND PROBATE

The simple reality is you can leave your money to whomsoever you want, be that to your family, your friends or to charities or other bodies. You can even confer one person in your family in preference to other family members or friends; it's your choice. Naturally, there are some ways in which this can be overruled, for example, by the Inheritance Act or '1975 Act', as mentioned above. This allows anyone who is a dependant at the time of your death and who has not been provided for in your Will to make a claim on your Estate. The list of who can make a claim against an Estate includes:

- A spouse or civil partner of the deceased
- A former spouse or civil partner of the deceased (who has not remarried or entered into another civil partnership)
- A child of the deceased
- Any person who, in relation to a marriage or civil partnership in which the deceased was at the time a party, was treated by the deceased as a child of the family (most commonly a stepchild)
- A person who was living in the same household as the deceased, as husband or wife, or as a civil partner of the deceased (most commonly known as a cohabitee) for a period of two years, with this two-year period ending immediately before the deceased's death
- Any person who immediately before the death of the deceased was being maintained either wholly

33

or partly by the deceased (ie someone financially dependent on the deceased)

Given the reasons covered above, it becomes clear why so many individuals decide that they have no need for a Will. They may feel safe in the knowledge that the law of intestacy will work perfectly well for them because, with their Estate left intestate, the rules can still result in their final wishes being carried out. For example, if a married individual with no children or grandchildren wishes for their spouse or civil partner to inherit their entire Estate, intestacy will deliver their wishes, so long as they are content for their spouse or civil partner to administer their Estate. Would they have benefited any better from writing a Will in that case? Perhaps so, if they overtly wanted to express their wishes and define in precise detail what would happen to their wealth once they passed away.

Conversely, it's perfectly legitimate for them to have considered that the expense and effort of preparing a Will was counterproductive, given that the law of intestacy would essentially deliver their final wishes. There are, however, no guarantees that your final wishes will be granted should you die intestate.

Example

A widowed man and a widowed woman marry. Each has two children from their first marriage, and they both accept their respective adult stepchildren. Crucially, though, they do not adopt their stepchildren as their own.

The husband dies first, leaving his entire wealth to his second wife under his Will, after which his second wife dies intestate. The rules of intestacy apply, and her two natural children inherit the whole Estate (namely, her Estate as well as her second husband's wealth). Her two stepchildren – his children – receive nothing.

In these circumstances, even though the husband and wife considered all four children to be equal, under the law of intestacy, the outcome based on their arrangements does not. The law simply reflected the blood relationship between the wife and her two children.

Had the wife declared her second husband's intentions by making a Will providing for her children and stepchildren alike, the upheaval and complications that intestacy can lead to would have been avoided. There is much to be said, therefore, for making a good Will, to ensure that goodwill between those we leave behind continues.

What makes a good Will?

Fundamentally, a good Will provides absolute clarity around what you want to happen to your money and your possessions after you die. The Will is also your chance to name your executors – the people that you trust to carry out your wishes on a competent basis.

For each individual, choosing one or more executors is a unique decision. For many people, this decision is not particularly arduous, given they enjoy a harmonious family relationship, whereby the administration of the Estate will also be straightforward. However, not all family relationships are harmonious. Tensions often exist between various family members and between generations, and further complications can arise where ex-spouses and children from previous relationships are involved. It can feel difficult to ensure every party is fairly represented, if indeed that is the intention. For someone who has been married a number of times, with children from each relationship, making a 'good' Will can seem an insurmountable task. Being appointed as an executor under those circumstances can feel like being invited to drink from a poisoned chalice.

When you appoint your executors, the fundamental, overriding point is to choose people you are confident will carry out your wishes. Given that being appointed as an executor can come with extremely onerous responsibility, I'm often asked if it's preferable to appoint professional executors, in particular if those executorships lead into trusteeships. The answer once again depends on the person's circumstances.

Where a fractious family environment exists, it can sometimes be helpful to appoint a person who is independent of that tension so that they can approach any issues with a sense of real objectivity. Also, where sometimes Estates can be incredibly complex (for example, involving large property holdings or business interests, or where a trust arrangement is contemplated under the Will), a lay executor will be placed under an undue amount of pressure to try to administer them.

The families I work with generally fall into one of two camps:

1. **They are open and honest with each other.** The administration of the Estate is expected to be a straightforward matter, and the parents want to make sure that their children understand the arrangements and are willing and happy to be appointed as executors.

2. **Disharmony, difficult relationships or tensions exist.** Often the children aren't even considered as executors because appointing one in preference to another would exacerbate the existing tensions. In these circumstances, the role of executor and/or trustee might fall to friends or professionals. The arrangements are then typically not shared with the successors, to avoid any difficult conversations or – even worse – a dispute during the lifetime of the testator.

Of course, it's not my place to suggest who will benefit from what. However, I find that asking 'Do you really want to be that harsh?' or 'Is that quite how you want to be remembered?' creates a moment to pause and reflect, and sometimes can even partially heal rifts between generations. The questions also generate some enlightening conversations around how to deal with a family dynamic or the destination of the wealth. Sometimes the key objective is to preserve a legacy, for example a family title or a highly prized art collection. As I have mentioned, the choice of executors depends on each family and their circumstances, while attempting to identify the appropriate beneficiaries. Value is not restricted simply to monetary terms; it carries emotional weight too.

Appointing guardians

In the tragic circumstances where both parents die when there are dependent children below the age of eighteen, who will look after their best interests? Unless the parents have appointed guardians, normally through a provision in their Wills, it will be the State that decides who will take care of their children. In the first instance, that would involve Social Services; and, ultimately, it could be a judge who makes that decision. You may therefore wish to think about what that might mean for your children's future and whether you would want Social Services or a judge to decide on your children's care.

How do you determine who should be your children's guardians? A good place to start is in drawing up a classic list of advantages and disadvantages to help you choose the right individuals to raise your children if you were no longer alive. I always suggest keeping in mind a substitute, just in case your initial choice proves to be unwilling to act as guardian or, indeed, is no longer available to do so.

Draw up a list of factors important to you in determining the suitability of family or friends to be your children's guardians. Questions you may wish to consider include:

- Are the potential guardian's moral, religious and political beliefs sufficiently aligned with your own?
- How well do you know their own family situation, and is it stable? If they are unmarried, is there a long-term partner? Are their children of similar age to your own?
- Do they have good parenting skills, and what are their views on child discipline?
- If they have children, what are their views on their children's current education? Also, in due course, what are the options for further education?
- Do they encourage their own children (if they have any) to have interests outside of school?
- If the potential guardian is not a parent, how much do you know about how they were raised by their parents? In all probability, this would

influence how they would act as parent to your children.

- Does the potential guardian live near to you, or would you be happy for your children to relocate?

- Does the potential guardian have sufficient financial resources to buy a larger house to accommodate your children, or is their house large enough already?

- Could they pay for raising your children themselves, or would they need financial support from the money you leave your children? Understanding how well they manage money will bring comfort to you that your inheritance would be used wisely until your children were mature enough to look after their own finances.

- If the potential guardian is elderly and possibly out of step with the younger generation, is that outweighed by their ability to afford to look after your children?

- What would happen if they died before your children reached the age of eighteen?

- Is the potential guardian too young and only interested in their own family? If so, will they lack the ability to invest emotionally in your children?

- If the potential guardian is a sibling of yours and in their own early adult development, will they resent the responsibility of looking after your children if they themselves intend to enter higher education or are just starting out in their career? Is it right for you to ask them to accept this responsibility?

Finally, it is essential that you ask the potential guardian (and the substitute guardian) if they are indeed willing to take on this role. This of course invites a meaningful conversation rather than a superficial comment in passing; otherwise, there will be a potential legal dispute waiting to happen. It would also be sensible to emphasise that, if they were to change their mind and no longer wish to act as guardian to your children, they should inform you of this at the earliest opportunity.

Once you have made your decision, write to the guardian and substitute guardian to confirm the arrangements you've made. Outline the arrangements to your family members and possibly also to your close friends.

Remember: while addressing this issue may seem daunting, the only factor that's of any real importance is who will take care of your children. Let me remind you that, in the event of both parents passing away and leaving behind dependants where no guardians have been nominated, it will fall to the State to act in the best interests of your children. Surely, in just about every case, it must be preferable to appoint a guardian in respect of minor children? After all, it's an overt expression of love and affection that you would want them to be looked after in the best way possible if you were no longer around to do it yourself.

Another important point to remember is that, just because you nominate someone to be your children's guardian, that person doesn't necessarily need to be the one that then looks after them. It simply means that you've made well-considered provision so that someone you trust wholeheartedly can decide who will. This nuance of the process of guardianship is not well known or considered, and knowing it can help inform the decision making immensely. I've known many situations where one set of grandparents have been appointed as guardians without the intention that they themselves will care for their grandchildren. Rather, they are best placed to assess the overall situation as and when required, and can then choose who will take over the children's day-to-day care.

Finally, anyone you nominate in your Will that you'd wish to appoint as guardians can be changed at any point by adding a Codicil – an additional legal document that allows changes to your Will rather than you needing to write a new one. Circumstances and people do change, so you never need to feel as if your Will is written in stone.

What a good executor looks like

There's a convention within executorships that is often described as the 'executor's year'. The expectation is that, within twelve months following the date of death, an executor should be able to submit the probate application, obtain the grant of probate, collect in the Estate, and be ready to provide a statement that accounts for everything they've received and how they propose to distribute it in accordance with your Will. The presumption is that, if they're not in a position to conclude the administration of the Estate within that timeframe, there needs to be an unequivocal explanation as to why it has not been possible. Sometimes that can be as a result of highly complex unresolved affairs or ongoing legal issues. The good executor will therefore be someone who is able to meet the standard required within that executor's year.

Not everyone wants to fulfil the role of executor, especially if they feel they don't possess the skills required or believe they aren't an excellent delegator. In those circumstances, provided the prospective executor hasn't become involved in the administration of the Estate, they can disclaim the role. There have been occasions when I've seen the role foisted maliciously on a family member, who has then – quite within their rights – repudiated the responsibility. Where no willing or available executor can be found, it will fall to another individual with the appropriate standing to apply for letters of administration.

Therefore, bear in mind that, if you've been named as executor, you are not required to fulfil the role as long as you declare your intention not to do so before becoming involved in managing the Estate. This is known as 'intermeddling', and you should be careful given how little it takes to find yourself as executor acting in an Estate.

Conversely, a bad executor or trustee creates delays and relies on subjective decisions that often manifest themselves in high-handed behaviour. Again, I've seen this happen all too often, when an executor or a trustee treats the role as if it were part of their personal fiefdom, resulting in beneficiaries losing trust and confidence. One particular case I was involved with, relating to a trust created to hold the wealth of the deceased, ended up before a judge when the trustee proclaimed that they were the only person left in the world able to carry out the wishes of the deceased. The four children and twelve grandchildren of the deceased disagreed, informing the court that the trustee was the *last* person they trusted. Within a matter of minutes, the judge made up his own mind and removed that individual from their fiduciary role.

I have more than once been appointed to act as trustee on the order of a High Court judge. In one case that was because a deceased husband had appointed an accountant as his co-trustee to manage a large trust fund. Unfortunately, it came to the attention of the deceased's wife and children that the trustee was investing disproportionate funds from the trust fund into a private company, which subsequently failed. The entirety of the investment was lost, but the trustee exhibited no sense of shame or remorse. Small wonder, then, that the widow and children lost all trust and confidence in this trustee and asked him to retire from his role. He refused to do so, no doubt influenced by the sizeable trustee fees he was drawing every year. Legal proceedings were instigated against him, he lost and was removed, and I was appointed as successor trustee.

3
What Do I Own?

Quite surprisingly, on a day-to-day basis, most people aren't fully aware of exactly what they own. They might have a sense of what their wealth is but usually not on a granular level. However, that viewpoint changes as soon as they turn their attention to dealing with the potential liabilities due in a prospective IHT calculation. At the point of their death, *everything* they own – either directly or indirectly – needs to be listed.

Clearly, it's advantageous if you do know what you own and how you own it. That might be because you are the beneficiary of a trust fund; or because you have interests in a financial structure such as a limited company that owns your business or a series of assets, be that 100% or otherwise. Factors such as these make a difference to the value that's included in your IHT return. Knowing this information will go a long way in helping you determine who should receive your wealth when you die.

The three key areas I will help you identify in this chapter are:

1. Financial structures

2. Trusts

3. Personal assets

The obligation on completing an IHT return is absolute – it has to be correct. The process might seem laborious, but when it comes to IHT, you cannot take a casual approach to evaluating what you own and what it is worth. Estimations are not enough – unless the items are trivial.

Someone – you or your advisor – will need to look carefully in each and every corner if you want to avoid significant problems down the line, either for you or for your successors. For the purpose of this book, I will therefore assume you are someone who is well ordered in your life and would want everything to be left neat and tidy.

Financial structures

Limited liability companies

If you have an interest in a limited liability company, you need to know how to distinguish between the shareholders in the company and the company itself and, in particular, what assets the company owns. In terms of IHT, this is important because you need to determine the value of your share interest, if not 100%, as any proportionate interest is normally valued at a discount to the total assets of the company such as any property.

You might then own shares in the company, and attached to those shares there may be a variety of rights and entitlements. It's worth noting, however, that not every share is created equal; some carry different entitlements and weight, depending on how they are structured, and their value may be dependent on what other people (shareholders and directors) within the company have agreed to. Ordinary shares, for example, are normally all created equally, which simplifies matters if that's the only class of shares that exist for that company. You might also have been offered preferential shares, which equate to a return on the amount invested and a prior charge, as a dividend, on the business's profits. In some instances, shares are deferred shares, which can be virtually worthless other than in exceptional circumstances.

Nobody said this would be easy, but the complexity of all the possible combinations in share ownership and values does require careful disentangling if you are to calculate potential IHT liabilities.

Partnerships

These are where a group of individuals agree to enter into a business, with a view to realising a profit together. The value of your interest in the partnership will normally be set out in the partnership agreement, which sets out your interest in the profits of the business – both trading profits and the share in any capital profits.

Limited liability partnerships (LLPs)

LLPs are similar to both limited liability companies and partnerships, in that they allow for a partnership structure where each partner's liabilities are limited. The main difference is that an LLP is an incorporated form of a partnership, protecting its members with limited liability in the event of insolvency.

From an IHT perspective, the value of your LLP share is, like for a partnership, usually set out in the members' agreement, which also sets out your interest in the profits of the business – both trading profits and the share in any capital profits.

Trusts and settlements

A trust (also known as a settlement) is a mechanism that has been widely used by families since Anglo-Saxon times. In many respects, its early foundations have remained largely intact. When a person – the settlor – establishes a trust, they give authority to a group of individuals – the trustees – to control and make decisions as to the administration and investment of the assets that lie within the trust fund. As a result, nominated individuals, charities or institutions – the beneficiaries – will enjoy these assets.

Trusts therefore involve three main parties:

1. **The settlor:** The person(s) whose assets are put into a trust

2. **The trustee:** The person(s) who manages the trust

3. **The beneficiary:** The person(s) who benefits from the trust

The legal duty of trustees is to administer and distribute the assets in the trust in accordance with the terms of the trust deed. At all times, the trustee must be seen to act in the best interests of the beneficiaries. In certain circumstances, the settlor may also be one of the trustees, and it's also possible for a beneficiary to be a trustee.

Typically, for IHT purposes, trusts are classified as either relevant property trusts, or non-relevant property trusts. There is a considerable difference between the two for IHT purposes:

1. **Relevant property trusts:** Any wealth held within a relevant property trust is not part of the testator's Estate for IHT purposes. Relevant property trusts are typically discretionary trusts but, following the reforms of Inheritance Tax on trust funds introduced in 2006, might also include life interest or interest in possession trusts.

2. **Non-relevant property trusts:** The value of the assets held within a non-relevant property trust are part of the testator's Estate and subject to IHT on their passing or transfer to another individual. Non-relevant property trusts are typically Life Interest Trusts created before the reforms of Inheritance Tax on trust funds introduced in 2006, and Life Interest Trusts for the surviving spouse created following a death after those reforms were introduced.

I explain more relating to the reforms of Inheritance Tax on trust funds introduced in 2006 in Chapter 9.

The main types of asset classes

Knowing exactly what assets make up your entire portfolio will have an impact on how you then deal with them for IHT purposes. My clients are often surprised when I tell them the assets they own, beyond the value of their home, will increase their IHT liability unless they make provisions to mitigate against this in their Will. Below I will describe some of the obvious and more surprising asset classes, ranging from the personal to the commercial, that individuals can plan for effectively so that their beneficiaries suffer less IHT and, ultimately, inherit more.

Residential properties

Essentially, these are the bricks and mortar that include your primary home, one or more secondary residences, overseas holiday houses, and any properties let out to third parties.

Commercial properties

Typically occupied by third parties – ordinarily, commercial property – these can comprise a portfolio of shops, offices and industrial buildings.

Agricultural property

This is typically land given over to arable or livestock farming. Also included are physical assets such as barns and farm-worker dwellings. Be aware, therefore, that if you own the cottages in which your farm workers live, the value of those cottages forms part of your Estate.

Forestry

Forestry can, surprisingly, take many forms. If you are growing trees for the purpose of deriving a profit from felling them, that land is typically regarded as commercially managed woodland and would be considered a business, thereby qualifying for IHT relief, as long as you have owned it for more than two years. At the other end of the spectrum are woodlands providing shelter to your home or a personally used land holding, which form part of your Estate.

Quoted stocks and shares

This is a portfolio of investments listed on a recognised stock exchange. Knowing your position fully, in respect of any type of shareholdings, is vitally important in calculating your potential IHT liability.

Unquoted stocks and shares

In respect of unquoted investments, it is not always straightforward to pass these on to your successors. Agreements can exist between the shareholders, which may preclude your successors from becoming future shareholders on your death, with your shares having to be offered to the remaining shareholders.

Digital assets

This is fast becoming an area that provokes much thought and debate, especially as to what digital assets are exactly and what value they hold or attract. Lack of clarity ranges from who owns your social media accounts to the use of cloud services to back up your photographs and documents, and there are questions around how this ownership passes on, if at all, as not all digital assets may be part of your Estate. There may be no monetary value involved, but what if it were you who captured that one image of the royal family that took the world by storm and earned you a significant global royalty? Would all that money then be lost upon your death? It's still an emerging area and one of great concern. Without complete access to all of your assets once you have passed away, this then presents a practical difficulty. It is therefore worth ensuring some means of others legitimately accessing your digital assets after you die.

Trophy assets

As with any asset class, there are costs associated with owning trophy assets. These costs often include substantial commissions on buying and selling assets, storage, insurance and maintenance, and increasingly careful consideration is needed to the legal, regulatory and tax perspectives.

Of course, one person's trophy can be another person's trinket. Trophy assets not only offer immense enjoyment to the owner, but they can also significantly appreciate in value over time (although they can lose value too). The potential downside is that they rarely generate income to cover their costs of ownership and can be a burden to the next generation when inheriting them.

These days, trophy assets can attract a greater degree of attention than they used to, thanks to popular TV programmes such as *Antiques Roadshow*. Trophy assets often represent scarcity. For example, when an artist dies, their body of work becomes finite (unless there is some later discovery of lost works, which can cause understandable excitement).

Items that typically can be classed as trophy assets include the following.

Classic cars

Owning a classic car with an impeccable provenance can represent the ultimate in trophy assets, often reflected by its value. An example is the Ferrari 250 GTO that sold for US$38.1 million (including buyer's premium) in August 2014. Not all classic cars command high prices, and often it's an individual's passion rather than the car's value that determines its pride of place in a collection. Broadly speaking, in the UK, most classic cars are exempt from Capital Gains

Tax when sold at a gain (and conversely, any losses are not allowed). For IHT purposes, the value of a car will form part of an individual's Estate if directly owned and will be subject to IHT unless qualifying for business property relief.

Firearms

In general, most firearms are exempt from Capital Gains Tax if they have a predictable life of less than fifty years. For IHT purposes, the value of a firearm will form part of an individual's Estate if directly owned, and the firearm will be subject to IHT unless used in the individual's business and qualifying for business property relief. In some families, firearms such as rifles and shotguns are an integral part of their land conservation activities or are retained simply for sporting purposes. They are often handed down from generation to generation or are purchased as a gift for younger generations. Shotguns are sometimes bought singularly and sometimes bought in pairs. Executors and their beneficiaries should take immediate steps to secure the storage of and obtain certificates to hold the firearms, including contacting the police regarding the gun licence.

Medals

Medals are often handed down through the generations and can be treasured family heirlooms. In some instances, they will be sold at auction and can fetch substantial sums as prized collectors' items. For IHT purposes, it's therefore advisable to obtain valuations before considering what is intended for the medals when you pass away; whether it is intended that they will be retained by the next generation, or it is probable they will be sold. If retained, their value will be exempt from IHT.

Antiquarian books

The marketplace for such books is at best unpredictable, but their value will still form part of your Estate for IHT purposes. Some books are highly valuable, such as *Audubon's Birds of America* – a rare nineteenth-century masterpiece, which became one of the world's most expensive published books when sold in 2010 for US$10.3 million.[7]

Literary papers

If you are a writer or a national figure, you should consider appointing a literary executor to deal with your works, ie for the disposal of copyright and to resolve any royalty issues. The value of your literary papers will be included in your Estate for IHT purposes, unless they are held as a part of your business,

---

7   G Levy, '*Birds of America*: The world's most expensive book sells for $10m at auction', *Time* (2010), https://newsfeed.time.com/2010/12/08/birds-of-america-the-worlds-most-expensive-book-sells-for-10m-at-auction, accessed 27 March 2023

in which case relief from IHT will be given as business property relief.

Artists' works

The work of an artist will often include not only finished and saleable works, but also the unfinished contents of any studio. The value of your artistic work will be included in your Estate for IHT purposes, but if held as a part of your business, relief from IHT will be given as business property relief.

Bloodstock

Thoroughbred horses (bloodstock) offer the potential for profit through prize money, and from breeding and selling your horses. The annual costs of keeping bloodstock can, however, be high.

Fine wines

Wine is normally purchased directly by an individual, most usually *en primeur* from a fine wine merchant, to be laid down for years before drinking. The sale of most bottles of wine are exempt from Capital Gains Tax if they have a predictable life of less than fifty years. The value of a wine collection will form part of an individual's Estate if directly owned and will be subject to IHT.

Jewellery

Often, individuals accumulate jewellery in their lifetime, either through gifts or inheritance. Jewellery can acquire a personal significance and become a family heirloom. It will still need to be valued if owned by an individual at the date of their death. The open market value can be significantly less than the insurance value.

Overview

I hope I have prompted you to consider that, for the purposes of IHT, you will easily be able to identify a large number of tangible assets and financial structures from which your successors may benefit, should you so choose, after you pass away. However, I have also broadened the scope so that you perhaps consider items and possessions that give you pleasure and enjoyment in life, irrespective of their monetary value.

No matter where your interests lie outside those areas that are financially quantifiable, there are numerous things on which we can't place a value, other than them being a reflection of us as individuals. You could assert that these too are priceless and that they say as much about us when we are gone, if not more so, than does the value of our Estates for IHT purposes.

4

Succession Planning For Your Business

Thinking about who will inherit your personal wealth and assets is one thing. Thinking about who will inherit your business interests is another.

For some parents, their business is so particular to themselves that the issue of succession planning simply may not be relevant. For others, succession planning presents an array of complex and emotional issues; an example might be where a business employs a large number of people and has a multimillion-pound turnover and a life beyond that of the owner. The parents may then see the business as their legacy – one they've developed from scratch or had passed down to them from the previous generation. In the latter case, succession planning is a relevant concern.

This chapter is not primarily concerned with explaining the IHT liabilities. Usually business property relief – at 100% of the value of the business – is available, as discussed in Chapter 6, meaning that no IHT is payable. Rather, this chapter is about determining who will inherit your business and who will take the future responsibility of managing it. With that in mind, I will describe various courses of action that result in successful succession planning. I will also outline a series of measures that the owner of a business can implement to secure that legacy for their family and for future generations.

Who should inherit your business and when?

In the early stage of a first-generation business, the ownership is closely controlled, sometimes within a single family. As it grows and becomes more profitable, the two areas the business owner should focus on are:

1. Who gets the value of the business
2. Who gets the responsibility for running the business

That may not necessarily be the same person or group of people for both. Some family members will work extremely hard for the business, while there may be siblings who, for whatever reason, don't. This should prompt the owner to focus on the management of the business – if the business were to cease operating properly, its value could soon be destroyed. It is therefore of paramount importance to resolve the management capabilities of the business going forward, since that will then offer security in respect of its future earnings. If those earnings are sustainable, it follows that the present value is similarly sustainable, with potential to grow further. At all costs, you want to avoid proving the saying true that 'The first generation grows the business, the second sustains it, and the third loses it'.

> **CASE STUDY: The Goodwood legacy**
>
> A family business that has managed its succession planning well is the Goodwood Estate, held by the Dukes of Richmond and Gordon.
>
> It was the tenth Duke who, with his son – then Lord March – in the 1990s revived the Estate's motor racing circuit. The circuit had previously been closed following several terrible accidents, most notably that involving Stirling Moss in 1962.
>
> Goodwood is now known for its motor racing, golf, horseracing and events; and since 2003, the Goodwood Estate has become home to one of the world's premier motor manufacturing brands, Rolls Royce. The family continues to manage the business with great success, under the continued leadership of Lord March, now the eleventh Duke. Many family

> business owners will recognise and share that entrepreneurial mindset, irrespective of the size of their own enterprise.[8]

It's important to understand that mindset: when a person establishes their business, they will progress though the classic cycle that begins with an idea that over time turns into a formative business, which then grows and becomes more substantial and self-sustaining. However, there comes a point when the business owner's mindset shifts from seeking continual growth and improvement to how that business can be passed on. Now, probably in their mid to late fifties, the owner has dedicated thousands of hours to growing the business and made any number of personal sacrifices in the process, including spending less time with their family. Their thoughts turn to succession planning and who will take on their mantle of running the business and building on their legacy. They will most likely seek someone who is younger, more energetic and full of promising ideas that have real potential to work out.

The business owner will no doubt have many questions, among which will be:

- Where do I begin?

---

[8] Goodwood, 'Freddie March – Driving Ambition' (Goodwood, 2018), www.goodwood.com/flying/latest-news/freddie-march---driving-ambition, accessed 27 March 2023

- What are the criteria?
- Who can I turn to for help?
- Who can I trust?
- What are the family issues that need dealing with?

Having devised this set of questions, the business owner would do well to form an advisory panel, drawn from people that currently work within the business as well as some that are external to it. The business owner would look to this advisory panel to help reach an objective assessment as to the most appropriate way forward.

If family members are appointed to senior roles, the business owner may want to ask themselves the simple question, 'If they weren't family members, would I appoint them to senior roles within the business?' The advantage of an independent advisory panel is that such assessments of the situation can result in sensible (and the right) choices, some of which may be difficult decisions to make, on a family member's suitability for a senior role. The answer may depend on whether the family member who is being groomed to enter the business has been encouraged to gain and has gained work experience outside of the family business. Otherwise, there's a risk the business can become insular and lack a wider perspective of the marketplace. The decision also depends on whether nominating a successor from within the family might be the worst possible outcome for that person or for the family as a whole.

Any decision to make an external appointment needn't result in the family not benefiting from involvement in the future running of the family business. However, in that scenario, any new CEO might well expect to hold an equity stake by way of incentivisation after a period of years, thus diluting the family shareholding. Different types of shares could be considered in the incentivisation arrangements. All such decisions should be considered and are, of course, unique to each family.

At its core, the question of who to nominate as successor relies on the business owner determining the right time for them to stop so that they can embark on a new chapter in the final part or parts of their life. Reaching that turning point ought to be predicated upon the business owner having something else to occupy them once they relinquish their day-to-day role in the business, even if that means retaining some level of emeritus position such as chair of the board or president of the company.

The importance of meticulous planning

Having made the decision that the right time to step aside is fast approaching, it's vital that the business owner is open and transparent with their family about their plans, to avoid unwelcome surprises when the owner is no longer present to explain or direct business affairs. The same principle must apply to the business itself, with the business owner outlining the intention to the external advisory board, who can then consider matters in totality. That should also involve someone who can be trusted enough to act as a critical friend, who is familiar with the financial and legal affairs of the business, and who will not hold back their opinions if they have any concerns or doubts about the financial running of the business. Equally as crucial will be discussing matters with that critical friend, who is not on the board of directors and who can offer unbiased advice on how the business could potentially be structured in the future. A family advisory board, therefore, plays a vital role in this consideration, and this should be augmented with a family constitution that sets out how the family should conduct themselves going forward in relation to the family business.

That constitution can then consider matters such as:

- Who will own the business
- Who will set policy
- Who will run the day-to-day management of the business

The constitution could also determine:

- Whether ownership should be open to all of the family
- What happens when some members wish to withdraw from ownership

- The policy surrounding remuneration from the business for family members who are part of the executive team
- The dividend policy to reward family member shareholders

The family constitution must also address how the business will achieve dispute resolution on a mutually agreeable basis, being fair to all parties, with the objective of avoiding litigation where nobody really wins.

The final point the constitution needs to consider is, where a case exists for the business to be sold, that a mechanism should be in place that respects the family decision. This might require exceeding a hurdle percentage rate of total ownership (obviously more than 50% and maybe as high as 75%) to decide whether the business is sold or retained. That mechanism crucially needs to provide the security by which any family members that disagree with such a decision must respect the consent of those who support it.

The unique and special nature of every family business means that each business owner will need to respond to only those points relevant to the business's makeup, relationships and vision for the future. Providing a framework for those discussions and approaching the issues raised above offers a business owner the opportunity to step outside of the ring and look back to its centre with a degree of objectivity in order to assess its potential future. Nothing will ever be satisfactorily achieved by sticking a finger in the air and trying to gauge from which direction the wind is blowing.

You may already be thinking it's approaching that time to have those conversations with yourself, your family and your advisors. They are the discussions that ultimately sit at the back of your mind and lead you to ask, 'Who will get my money when I die?' If wealth has been generated by your business, that will create the legacy you wish to pass down to your successors. Assuming you have a properly funded pension scheme in place, or if you have accumulated independent wealth outside of your business, you will have ensured financial independence from the business during your retirement, thus also protecting your spouse in the process. Any capital released to you at the time of sale will, of course, attract a tax liability. That capital may further expose you to a greater IHT liability if it remains within your Estate, unless you intend to spend it during your retirement.

How far in advance to start planning to pass the business on

As I've mentioned above, this will depend entirely on when you are ready to pass the business on, which could conceivably be at any stage in your lifetime. However, the most fantastic opportunity might arise where, for example, a third party is keen to buy and expand your business into markets you've only ever dreamed of. Who knows – that might well be the best offer you'll receive and can allow someone else to take your business to another level. Conversely, yours might be the kind of business that's so associated with you and your personality that you need to let it run the course of your lifetime.

Whatever prompts your decision to sell, that will be the moment you feel you want to stop working in favour of taking on a new challenge – maybe even retirement. Even if you're wondering whether it's a good idea to pass the business on to the family, the answer could be debatable. The decision will depend on whether the next generation possess the right skillset, because you'll want to avoid handing down a poisoned chalice and seeing the value of the business destroyed or your family's outlook on life harmed. Your intention will be that it's an opportunity to be a life-enhancing experience, not a noose around their neck. Clear alternatives are to sell the business to a third party or to close it and sell its assets and customer database. No matter which way you proceed, it's still a personal decision.

For argument's sake, assuming you decide to pass on the business to your children, how do you share ownership among them? In fact, there are two straightforward options:

1. Transfer a shareholding into their own names, which clearly defines what they are entitled to and when.
2. Set up a trust fund that owns the shareholding.

What if your preferred nominated successor isn't ready to take control?

As mentioned, you can appoint someone outside of the family who can run the business. In the interim, your proposed successor can understudy them for a number of years until they are ready to assume leading the business. Handling this with sensitivity and respect to the de facto leader is key to generating results – it wouldn't be ideal to appoint an acting CEO simply to force them out ten years later when your child is finally ready to step into your shoes.

Who you choose as your successor remains your decision, but consider carefully whether they'll ensure that your values will continue once you move away from the business.

> **CASE STUDY: Upside-down**
>
> John Timpson, founder of the eponymous chain of 2,000 Timpson stores across the UK, handed control of his empire to his son, James, in 2002.

> To this day, James continues his father's well-known 'upside-down' style of management, which has been key to the growth of the business.[9]

The approach – or response – to who will get your money when you die will vary depending on your individual circumstances. The factors considered in this chapter include relationships, dependencies on others, and individual responsibilities, their developing maturity and the accumulation of wealth. Each new stage has its typical concerns, activities and problems that normally add to rather than totally replace the previous stage. Most importantly, the stages are normally undertaken successively.

Perhaps now is the very time for you, having already achieved everything you have thus far, to ask yourself, 'What do I want?'

---

9 Investec, 'The remarkable transformation of a British retail dynasty' (Investec, 2020), www.investec.com/en_gb/focus/business-growth/remarkable-transformation.html, accessed 27 March 2023

PART TWO
THE FUNDAMENTALS OF IHT PLANNING

The key points in the following chapters will help you understand that, with the benefit of full knowledge of the building blocks of IHT planning, you will make better decisions for yourself and for those who will inherit your money.

It is vital that you can quantify what your potential IHT liability would be on your death. Knowing that information could well have a significant impact on your decisions on who gets your money when you die. This is especially true if you presume that an IHT liability will automatically arise when you die, when in fact, there may be no IHT liability, or it may be much less than you expected.

Such incorrect assumptions can, and do, lead to poor and unnecessary decisions, which then result in poor outcomes, all for the want of full and complete professional advice. Conversely, in circumstances where a large IHT liability is unavoidable, this too can be problematic. On the other side of the coin, family members now face the possibility of disposing of treasured assets, including property and heirlooms, in order to meet death duties. Neither outcome is ideal, but these considerations demonstrate the significant advantage of knowing in detail what you actually own before making any hasty evaluation of how to leave your Estate. It's important to not only understand that IHT planning isn't simply an IHT calculation of what's payable on your death. It's also about understanding the fundamentals of IHT planning, including:

1. Making effective lifetime gifts to individuals and surviving the seven years

2. Using the valuable exemptions to pay no IHT

3. Knowing which assets qualify for 100% relief from IHT (typically agricultural and business property)

4. Placing assets into trust for future generations (typically your family)

5. Building up funds that are not aggregated with your Estate (such as pension funds)

6. Using life assurance to help pay any IHT

PART TWO: THE FUNDAMENTALS OF IHT PLANNING

Once you understand these fundamentals, IHT will not become an unwelcome, unpleasant issue that needs to be dealt with at the time of your death. Rather, it's an issue that can be planned for with multiple, generous solutions, some of which can be enjoyed during your lifetime, which give you reassurance that IHT will not be such an onerous problem for your loved ones.

Throughout Part Two, I will describe how Inheritance Tax can become payable on your wealth, and the steps you can take, both in lifetime and on death, to make that tax liability a voluntary tax liability.

5
Avoiding The Bear Traps Set By HMRC To Defeat Your IHT Planning

Failing to properly implement your IHT planning will invariably open up your affairs to the strictest scrutiny. There are a number of ways in which HMRC tries to defeat your IHT planning, and it is not shy to legislate in its favour. However, responsible tax planning continues to be permitted, even if publicly the increasingly held view is that it is the duty of all taxpayers to pay their fair share of tax.

This chapter will explain several of the more common bear traps set by HMRC, which can be painful and punitive if you fall into them. I will explain the legislation aimed at specific areas of perceived tax avoidance, for example, gifts with reservation of benefit legislation. I will also outline legislation aimed at general avoidance.

Gifts with reservation of benefit – the GWROB rules

HMRC will always seek clarification on whether you disposed of significant assets properly during your lifetime. They will want to know if the documentation provided upon your death accurately represent your assertions in respect of your wealth in your lifetime. In particular, they will want to be reassured you have not fallen foul of the GWROB rules, whereby a person might give away their assets in such a way that the enjoyment of the property given away is not fully assumed by the donee.

Examples

1. A parent gifts their main house to their adult child, with a view to living in a separate, smaller cottage they also own nearby. They keep ownership of the cottage, and yet they continue to treat the main house as if it is still their primary residence, for example, holding social events and parties in that house, despite purporting to having given it away. The reality here is that the possession and enjoyment of the property given away is not fully assumed by the donee because the parent continues to use it. The house will therefore be considered to be a GWROB.

2. A parent purports to gift an art collection to their children. In fact, the collection remains in the parent's residence, without any rental consideration

for its use paid over to their children. That would clearly not represent a gift for IHT purposes as it would fall within the GWROB rules.

We might all be tempted to wonder how HMRC might possibly know any of this, given that Orwell's vision of the UK hasn't quite come to pass. It's a good question, but to some extent, the answer is not only a moral one – it is backed up by the force of law in England and Wales. That's because the executors, who file the IHT return for the deceased, are obliged to make full and proper enquiries as to the value of their Estate. This includes assets that are given away in a person's lifetime and whether the deceased retained any benefit from those assets.

Furthermore, if executors fail to make those full and proper inquiries, HMRC could subsequently prove that this was a GWROB. The inheritors of the Estate would then, through the executors, find themselves paying penalties on the under-declared IHT amount as well as the IHT itself, plus late payment interest.

For the GWROB rules to apply, the relevant period is anytime between the original gift and the GWROB ceasing within the seven years before the donor's death. All that is required is that the benefit resumes at any point in this period and the value of the property at the date of death is brought back into the IHT Estate of the donor on their death.

Why caution is needed

The GWROB rules are without doubt penal in nature. Not only do they bring back into an IHT charge the value of an asset at its open market value at the date of death, even if the asset was gifted at a much lower value many years previously. This bringing back into the IHT charge can apply not only if the retained benefit is held at the time the donor dies, but also if the retained benefit is given up in the seven years before the donor dies. The IHT liability is then payable by the donee, whose base cost in regards to Capital Gains Tax remains at the date of gift, not at the date of death or at the date the reservation of benefit ceases.

Similarly, the pre-owned assets tax (POAT) rules were introduced by HMRC as a tax charge on money that had been given away and which didn't fall within the scope of IHT upon a person's death as a GWROB. A classic example is where money is given away by parents to their children but is then 'recycled' in such a way that their children purchase a house that their parents go on to occupy. In this instance, the donor is then deemed to have a benefit on the provision of the house, which is then subject to an income tax charge, unless the donor accepts that the value of the house is within their IHT Estate.

The POAT rules were designed for IHT purposes to tackle the "home loan scheme" – an IHT-avoidance scheme, whereby an individual reduced or removed the value of their home from their Estate, while continuing to live rent-free during their lifetime. The POAT rules, however, have a much wider application and show the level of detail HMRC expects from executors in completing the IHT return.

As the following example shows, GWROBs are harmful to your financial health.

Example

In 1990, when Robert gifted his son an original artwork by a then relatively unknown artist, it was valued at £25,000. Over the years, the value of contemporary art has significantly appreciated.

When Robert reaches his seventieth birthday, he asks his son if he can hang the contemporary picture in his home for the month during which he is hosting several parties to celebrate this milestone in his life. His son agrees and understandably does not ask his father to pay any rent to hang the picture in his home.

Two years later, the artist dies, which leads to a major retrospective of their work in the Metropolitan Museum of Modern Art. Consequently, the value of the work skyrockets.

Sadly, Robert dies three years later with a large Estate for IHT, including the painting he gave to his son, which is now worth a staggering £225,000. This turns out to be a tax disaster. The IHT liability is now £90,000, payable by his son, who doesn't have the funds to settle this liability. He in turns sells the painting, realising a capital gain of £200,000, on which up to £40,000 of Capital Gains Tax is payable. Robert's son is left with £95,000, but of course, any financial gain here is outweighed by the emotional capital lost in having to sell his father's precious heirloom.

The situation baffles the family, especially because the painting was gifted to Robert's son so many years ago. The result is unequivocal, though – the painting falls under the GWROB rule, since the seven-year period runs from when the reservation ceased, namely during Robert's seventieth year of celebrations.

Other points to note about GWROB are:

- Its rules only apply in respect of gifts made on or after 18 March 1986. The GWROB rules are not retrospectively applied to gifts before that date.

- If full consideration is paid (see below), there is no reservation of benefit from the gift. If partial consideration is paid, there can be no gift of the part paid for. It is only when there is a reservation of benefit that there can be a GWROB.

- If the heirloom subject to the GWROB rules is sold, the reservation to the donor ceases at the moment of sale. Cash gifts settled into trust can be a GWROB if the heirloom comprised in the settlement represents, or is derived from, the gifted cash.

- There is a let-out from the effects of the GWROB rules if, for example, the gifted property is enjoyed virtually to the entire exclusion of the donor.

- The GWROB rules do not apply to exempted gifts for IHT purposes, including small gifts and those made in consideration of marriage, to charities and political parties, to maintenance funds and employee trusts, or for national purposes and public benefit.
- The GRWOB rules generally do not apply to gifts to spouses.

One effect of the GWROB rules is that a number of 'shearing' operations have been implemented to reduce IHT liability. Shearing refers to retaining a lesser interest in a more valuable asset.

Two examples of shearing arrangements considered to be effective for IHT purposes are:

1. The donor gives away shares in a company while continuing to receive remuneration. It is said that the continuation of reasonable remuneration arrangements is unlikely to be a GWROB in the shares gifted as a prior independent right, provided the work undertaken is reasonable for the remuneration received.

2. In a partnership business, the donor is entitled to a nominated percentage of both income profits and surplus assets. For example, where that is 70%, the partnership agreement is amended so that the share in surplus assets is reduced to 60%

but the share of income profits continues at 70%. The share of the income profits is also a prior independent right and so is not a GWROB.

These shearing arrangements allow commercial arrangements to be made in relation to family business interests that are effective for IHT purposes. They also allow older generations of a family to remain remunerated for their work and to offer their wisdom to younger generations of a family who have succeeded them.

The general anti-abuse rule (GAAR)

One of the more obscure rules that ideally should be avoided, namely the GAAR, was introduced to counter tax planning that Parliament considers to be egregious. There are typically hallmarks with such tax planning, where a promoter of a scheme creates a standard set of documents, which are then applied to an individual's circumstances. The promoter receives a premium fee, under the guise of a confidentiality agreement, which prevents any public discussion about what is being proposed.

The very fact this planning is shrouded in faux – or actual – secrecy should raise an immediate red flag. If you find HMRC is invoking the GAAR, you should immediately seek specialist advice.

Debts not repaid after death

Debts are normally deductible from an Estate in calculating its IHT liability, but there are certain circumstances where this will not occur. The starting assumption, therefore, is that all third-party liabilities will be repaid and that HMRC will make no enquiries as to their payment.

There are, however, occasions when beneficiaries assume the debt liabilities of the deceased when they take over their business interests, agreeing with lenders to the continuation of any outstanding loan facilities. This may be particularly so in relation to jointly held property where the loan facilities are on a joint and several basis, as between the deceased and the beneficiaries.

Debts owed to a borrower are also non-deductible for IHT purposes if the debt consisted of property previously gifted by the deceased to the borrower. The obvious circularity of the transactions is caught, and tax relief is denied.

Example

A parent gives his child £250,000. At a later date, he borrows back £200,000 from his child. When the parent dies, the debt of £200,000 has not been repaid.

The debt of £200,000 is then not deductible for IHT purposes in the parent's Estate.

Agricultural property or business property relief

When an individual raises a mortgage secured on their home to purchase property eligible for agricultural or business property relief (which, after two years, would qualify for 100% relief from IHT), that mortgage is now deducted from the property purchased rather than the individual's home.

Example

Bob raises an interest-only mortgage on his home so that he can purchase some farmland, which he then rents to a local farmer.

Bob dies three years later, leaving the mortgage unpaid. The mortgage is deducted from the value of the farmland before agricultural property relief is allowed in the IHT calculation.

In practical terms, the mortgage does not attract relief from IHT, but any increase in the value of the farmland does at least escape IHT.

Challenges to whether your IHT planning has been properly implemented

Ensuring that all the formalities for transferring or gifting significant property have been executed correctly is vitally important; otherwise, the consequences may be disastrous. Failing to complete the necessary legalities may result in all your good tax objectives and intentions falling at the first hurdle after you die.

The way in which a gift can be properly effected and remain unchallenged will depend on the nature of the gifted property. There are essentially three methods:

1. **By deed:** There are few transfers that need to be completed by deed. An example of one that does is the transfer or creation of an interest in land. Deeds have certain formalities to follow, such as signatures being witnessed, and that the deed has to be delivered (where the delivery may be actual, constructive or symbolic) in order for it to be effective.

2. **In writing:** This is necessary for certain transfers of assets such as the benefit of a contract, the transfer of shares and the transfer of most intellectual property rights. It's also advisable in all other circumstances so that there is a written record of the gift.

3. **By delivery or possession:** The title to chattels (goods and items) can pass by delivery, but simply telling someone you have made a gift is not sufficient and provides no real evidence. Where chattels are gifted by delivery, it is advisable to create written evidence, to avoid any suggestion against the necessary formalities having been completed.

> **CASE STUDY: The missing manuscript**
>
> A celebrated example of issues around delivery or possession occurred when the author Dylan Thomas lost the original manuscript of his radio play, *Under Milk Wood*. He told his producer at the BBC of a number of places the manuscript might be and allegedly said, 'If you can find it, you can keep it.' The producer tracked down the manuscript to a Soho public house, by which time Thomas had died.
>
> In the subsequent litigation with the executors of Thomas's Estate, it was held that the BBC producer was entitled to keep the manuscript as a completed gift. In legal terms, when the manuscript was found, Thomas had already released it into the possession of the producer.[10]
>
> If the producer had obtained written permission from Thomas, any legal wranglings might have been avoided.

There are lessons to learn from all of the above. Where formalities cannot be completed within the required timeframe, the alternative is for the donor to make a declaration of trust over the relevant property. Other problems that can arise include the non-simultaneous signing of documents by a required date, which cannot lawfully be rectified with back-dated signatures.

---

10 K Haas, 'A writer walks out of a bar… without his manuscript' (Rosenbach, 2014), https://rosenbach.org/blog/a-writer-walks-out-of-barwithout-his, accessed 27 March 2023

Similarly, the advance signing of draft documents cannot lawfully result in the execution of a complete and amended final version; there must always be an agreed version of the final version, which is circulated to all parties before signature. Otherwise, such documents are invalid and the purported transaction void, with the result that the gift has effectively not taken place.

Issues that arise when valid IHT planning is undone, by transfer made without proper authority, can also cause untold problems.

Example

Acting under a power of attorney, the son-in-law of an incapacitated man made gifts out of surplus income (as, genuinely, his father-in-law did not need the money, and such gifts were in accordance with his wishes) and, when his father-in-law died, claimed the exemption for normal expenditure out of income in the IHT return, as set out in Chapter 9.

It was held that the son-in-law, in his capacity as attorney, did not have the legal power to make gifts without approval from the Court of Protection. Accordingly, the amount claimed to have been gifted became an amount repayable to the father-in-law's Estate by the recipients of those so-called gifts.

As an amount owed to the Estate, the amount formed a part of the IHT Estate of his father-in-law at the date of death and was subject to IHT. If, however, the gifts had been validly made with the authority of the Court of Protection, the conditions for the normal expenditure out of income exemption would have been met.

The 'great escape' from HMRC by paying full consideration

Paying full consideration for the use of assets gifted, where a reservation of benefit has been retained, means that the Estate escapes IHT as there is then no GWROB. For example, a person could choose to give away their home to their children but continue residing at the property in return for rent. There is then no gift with reservation of benefit, and the IHT tax planning is supremely successful. Similarly, where a parent chooses to gift a valuable collection of artworks to their children while still enjoying the pleasure of them within their house, the parent can pay rent for the artworks. The value of the paintings thereby escapes IHT on their death because full consideration has been paid. Remember, though, that seven years usually has to elapse before the gift is fully out of your IHT Estate, although in some cases a shorter period can apply. Full consideration is therefore a simple and efficient means of future damage control. However, as I am about to describe below, sometimes it's difficult to limit the damage that arises as the result of injustices that are inherent within the IHT system.

The risk factor of IHT injustices

Unexpected tragedy can often result in a number of injustices. In truth, these injustices are not deliberate ploys on the part of HMRC that set out to cause untold misery to grieving relatives in their time of mourning. However, they do show how more planning or aforethought might ameliorate what has become a difficult time for any family to deal with.

Sadly, but fortunately rarely, I will be presented with a scenario where both a husband and wife have lost their lives as the result of an accident, most often as a result of a car crash. Fortunately, in most instances their children either were not with them at the time or survived the accident. Where the parents' wealth exceeds the available exemptions, at the very moment their young dependants need as much support as possible (both emotionally and financially), HMRC steps in and takes its share of their money through an IHT liability. That is quite an injustice.

Another circumstance I've often seen is where two elderly siblings choose to live together in their retirement, both having previously lived and worked independently of each other. They jointly own their new residence, but the property exceeds the value of IHT exemptions available to them. When one of the siblings dies, the surviving sibling can't afford to pay the IHT due on the value of a house, so the home has to be sold in order to pay the IHT. This is another injustice.

The last laugh?

In this chapter I wanted to raise your awareness to the fact that, if you stumble blindly through life without taking the necessary precautions, there are a number of nasty bear traps waiting to bite down hard on your wealth when you die. For those left to deal with your affairs, that can truly be a painful and punitive experience.

In particular, I wanted you to be aware that the most common HMRC traps people fall into are the rules concerning gifts with reservation of benefit (GWROB) and dealing with debts after death. It's also essential that any gift you make (or intend to make) can be accurately evidenced, since verbal testimony will not suffice post death.

I've also pointed out that injustices can occur where surviving family members are seemingly penalised in being saddled with significant IHT liabilities. This is not a suggestion that taxation is not a force for good in society. It's just that sometimes the heavy hand of the law often hits people harder when they are down, unless they seek the appropriate professional advice. However, I take some comfort in the fact that there are ways to circumvent potential injustices, and I'm happy to end this chapter with an example.

> **CASE STUDY: The generation game**
>
> When the legendary British variety entertainer, Sir Bruce Forsyth, died in August 2017, many people were surprised by an apparent injustice towards his six children in respect of his Will.
>
> Despite an Estate reportedly valued at £11.5 million, Sir Bruce left the vast majority to his wife, Wilnelia, while his six children were not named as beneficiaries and therefore received nothing. However, the star's reasoning was more an astute decision than any apparent slight towards his offspring.
>
> Sir Bruce would have been fully aware that there would be a substantial IHT liability to settle on his death, unless he made provision to avoid paying this 'voluntary' tax. Leaving his Estate to his wife and benefiting from the spouse exemption meant no IHT would be payable. This action essentially saved his Estate (and, therefore, his children) having to settle an unwelcome IHT bill. His surviving spouse would then be free to make gifts to his children without paying tax on them, utilising the rules for potentially exempt transfers. If Wilnelia survives the seven years from the date of the gifts, the amount given to his six children will also escape any IHT liability.[11]

My advice to you is to know what you own, think ahead and plan properly, to be sure you avoid falling into any of the bear traps I've described in this chapter.

---

11 J Badcock, 'How Bruce Forsyth played his cards right with inheritance tax', *The Times* (2018), www.thetimes.co.uk/article/how-bruce-forsyth-played-his-cards-right-with-inheritance-tax-fdk5rdhql, accessed 27 March 2023

6
Assets On Which No IHT Is Due

The tax reliefs for agricultural and business property are two of the most valuable available for reducing your IHT liability, as they can reduce the value of your taxable Estate by up to 100% of the relevant property. Any individual who owns a business or agricultural property will usually, though not necessarily, enjoy an active management role in the business in either case. Careful consideration is therefore needed as to how these businesses are to be run after the owner has died.

This chapter will focus on three specific areas of interest where understanding what those reliefs are, and how they can be applied, offers advantages from planning with care and aforethought to anyone undertaking IHT Estate planning. These areas are:

1. **Agricultural property:** The good news is that owning agricultural property in the UK attracts exemption from IHT, usually at the full 100%. The social purpose of this is to maintain continuity for significant landholdings and to minimise disruption upon an owner's death. The alternative proposition would be that, for every generation, the land, property and business interests would be sold or downsized each time an individual landowner died. We can see the disadvantages of that alternative from examples in continental Europe and further afield, where, through the rules of forced heirship, landholdings become ever smaller and thus consequently less viable as units.

2. **Business property:** In respect of a business, IHT property relief is also set at 100% relief for the value of the business, whether the business is UK based or held worldwide. Similar to agricultural property relief, the social purpose is to keep businesses intact so that they can seamlessly continue to support the economy and contribute towards the country's growth. In the event of the death of an owner, if a business had to be closed or a part of the business had to be sold off because of IHT, the social purpose of sustaining and growing the economy would be defeated.

3. **Pensions:** Nearly all of us are encouraged to save for our retirement, hence the various schemes and funds available that allow us to

accumulate money within pension funds that supplement the State pension provision. These private pensions can escape IHT on your death, although other tax charges can apply, depending on the value of your pension scheme and your age when you die.

In a sense, aside from the IHT relief advantages, I like to think of each of the above not only as planning for the inevitable finality we will all face. They are also a means by which we can maintain and strengthen those lines of continuity that serve a purpose beyond our own immediate family circles. This is especially because so often other families are also dependent on the individuals who have died.

The idea that the State might hold a similar opinion may come as a surprise to anyone who regards HMRC's scrutiny – and then taxation – of our Estates as an activity that lacks basic humanity. I'm not suggesting the IHT regime doesn't have its faults, but I'm always at pains to point out that IHT is the one tax over which we can have some degree of control, as long as we plan carefully in advance.

The four areas I cover in this chapter are ones that can impact far and wide should that planning fall short. There is something almost uplifting in the thought that death can, in fact, have influence over a social purpose long after we are gone. It's that diametrically opposed contrast in the fabric of our society – in the

UK especially – that is often maligned without considered justification. Irrespective of the disparity between people's personal situations – their wealth and their standing in society – there is little doubt that a far wider social good is derived from the facilities offered by the IHT relief and exemptions than if they didn't exist at all. That, for me, offers a wider perspective on precisely why we need to plan our IHT liabilities with as much care and attention to detail as we can – not simply for ourselves and those we love, but for all of us at large.

Agricultural property relief

It's important to understand where tax legislation boundaries begin and end within the scope of agricultural property relief. In general, this scope relates to:

- Agricultural property (ie lands and pasture)
- Ancillary woodland, or any buildings used for rearing of livestock or fish
- Farm buildings – for example, owner-occupied farmhouses and farm employee dwellings associated with the property

The critical qualifier for agricultural property relief is always the agricultural land, although the detail can appear baffling at first glance.

ASSETS ON WHICH NO IHT IS DUE

> **Example**
>
> A large country house that sits in the centre of fifty acres on which sheep are grazed is unlikely to qualify for agricultural property relief.
>
> The same large country house is likely to qualify for agricultural property relief if it sits – and serves – over a thousand acres where crops are grown.
>
> In other words, it's the difference between a rich man's house and a working farmhouse.

The contentious areas with agricultural property relief typically are:

- Relief for the agricultural value of the agricultural property
- The 'character appropriate' test in relation to buildings
- The definition of a farmhouse
- When the agricultural property is occupied for agricultural purposes
- 100% or 50%

Agricultural property considerations

Often, the owner of agricultural property considers that it is the open market value of the property that should attract agricultural property relief. However, agricultural property relief applies only to the *agricultural* value, which is the value where the land is subject to a perpetual covenant prohibiting its use other than as agricultural property. The discount to be applied will vary on the specific facts of each case. That said, the owner should get business property relief on the excess.

Once farmland is owned, there is a further presumption that all buildings on the farmland should qualify for agricultural property relief. While there is usually little controversy relating to farm buildings used for the purposes of agriculture, in contrast, the circumstances of the farmhouse are normally closely examined. However, the boundaries for relief are clear and serve proper purpose. Anyone employed as a herdsman or livestock manager on a large working farm knows that theirs is hardly a run-of-the-mill, nine-to-five job similar to that of an office worker. It's an around-the-clock responsibility, where they may at any time be called out, for example to attend to the welfare of the animals under their care or respond to a husbandry emergency caused by adverse weather. It's not unusual, therefore, for the landowner to provide such employees with accommodation on the farmland. Relief on those dwellings is sensibly granted to its fullest extent on the death of the landowner in order for that business to continue without any operational disruption. It's why farms are passed down from generation to generation, with the objective that each successive generation will also take on the business.

In respect of the actual bricks-and-mortar farmhouse on the land, a number of factors are therefore taken into consideration for agricultural property relief purposes:

- Whether the house is proportionate in size and nature to the requirements of the farming activities conducted on the agricultural land or pasture in question
- Even if it's not immediately discernible that a farmhouse satisfies the 'character appropriate' test, that it is obvious it has that purpose
- Whether the property is regarded as a house with land or farmland with a house
- How long the house in question has been associated with the agricultural property, and where there is evidential history of agricultural production
- Whether the farm provides a living for an individual who has bought the whole Estate

Acquiring farmland is also increasingly appealing to people who have attained their wealth in entirely different business areas and wish to diversify in their next phase of life by investing into a different class of assets.

> **CASE STUDY: Dyson's farm**
>
> Technology business entrepreneur Sir James Dyson now owns an enterprise, Beeswax Dyson Farming, which has helped him become one of the UK's biggest farmers. The enterprise is valued at over £0.5 billion, as reported by *Farmer's Weekly*, with around 35,000 acres of farmland in Sir James's ownership.[12]
>
> The principal areas of the business are:
>
> - Farming
> - Renewable energy
> - Estate (including rentable residential and commercial properties and woodland management)

I find this example interesting – an ultra-high-net-worth individual has made a series of calculated decisions, the impacts of which will mitigate some of the IHT issues his Estate will inevitably encounter at some point. For anyone with Dyson's wealth, the 'easy' option would simply be to acquire a large country house with acres of grounds, forming a pleasing residence. In essence, though, that form of ownership would not attract automatic IHT relief. However, the property does qualify for IHT relief if it is situated on a substantially larger acreage of agricultural land,

---

12 A Meredith, 'Dyson farming empire now worth more than £500m', *Farmers Weekly* (2019), www.fwi.co.uk/business/dyson-farming-empire-now-worth-more-than-500m, accessed 27 March 2023

because the farming enterprise would then be run by the farmer from the house itself. The relief itself doesn't require the owner to be working on a full-time business in the farm, as long as they are the farmer.

100% or 50%?

One other thorny issue for agricultural property owners is in determining whether agricultural property relief will be granted at 100% as opposed to 50%. To help explain the complexities, it's useful at this point to understand the legal context of farming tenancies in England and Wales.

Tenancies created under the Agricultural Holdings Act (AHA) 1986 allow agricultural holdings to be let by the landowner to a tenant. This allows tenants that have invested the necessary security (for example, to allow crops sufficient time to grow) in their property to realise the return on investment.

The tenant with an AHA tenancy may also be entitled to pass down their tenancy to their nominated successors (spouse, civil partner, sibling, child, or any person treated as a child of the tenant) upon their death. However, from the landowner's point of view, tenancies granted before 1 September 1995 attract agricultural property relief at 50% for the landowner. If the land is farmed by the landowner themselves, then 100% relief will be available.

In contrast, relief is available at 100% for land let on a farm business tenancy after 1 September 1995. In some cases, it may be possible to convert a pre-1995 tenancy into a new tenancy and secure the 100% relief for the landowner; this is worth considering for anyone looking to maximise their agricultural property relief.

In all cases, it should be remembered that there is a two-year ownership and occupation requirement where relief at 100% is available for land farmed in hand, and a seven-year occupation period where 50% relief is available for land farmed by a tenant.

Business property relief

Business property relief at either 100% or 50% can be granted on your business assets, which can be passed on either during your lifetime or as part of your Will. Business is defined as any form of ownership or share of a business, be that a sole trader, a partnership, or shares in a limited liability company. Usually, a business owner can expect to be granted business property relief at 100%. In some circumstances, however, business property relief is granted at 50%.

In general, the lower rate of 50% would apply to:

- Shares controlling more than 50% of the voting rights in a listed company

ASSETS ON WHICH NO IHT IS DUE

- Land, buildings or machinery that was owned by the deceased and used in a business they controlled or were a partner in
- Land, buildings or machinery used in the business and held in a trust from which the business has the right to benefit

It's worth noting that business property relief is only granted if the deceased owned the business or asset for at least two years before they died.

Business property relief is *not* available if the company is:

- In the process of being sold, unless to another company that intends to continue with the business and where the Estate is to be paid mostly in shares
- Being wound up, with the exception that this enables the business of the company to continue
- Predominately trading in securities, stocks or shares, property, or in making (or holding) investments
- A not-for-profit business

Furthermore, it's not possible to claim business property relief on an asset if or to the extent that it:

- Also qualifies for agricultural property relief
- Is no longer required by the business for use in the future
- Hasn't been used by the business in the main for the two years prior to it being passed on, either as a gift or as a bequest

The minor exception is that any part of a non-qualifying asset that is used in the business might qualify for business property relief. For example, if only one room in a retail unit is used for trading purposes and the remainder for residential, only the retail portion will qualify for business property relief.

In respect of gifts: a person can give away assets or business property during their lifetime and still attract business property relief, but only if the property or assets qualify and the recipient that wants to keep the relief maintains them as going concerns until the donor dies. A gift made more than seven years before the donor's death won't count towards their Estate for IHT purposes, unless brought back into account as a GWROB.

Business property relief is also granted if:

- The business or asset was owned by the donor for at least two years prior to it being gifted
- The business owner needs to replace the property or assets with something of equal value for use in the business, such as machinery or parts

CASE STUDY: Ineos

In 1998 business entrepreneur Sir Jim Ratcliffe formed INEOS (INspec Ethylene Oxide and Specialities), having bought up BP's ethylene oxide and glycol businesses.[13] The business soon flourished and made new acquisitions from other giants, including BASF and ICI. Today, the global annual revenue of INEOS is now £65 billion.[14]

Because he is a major shareholder in that business, Ratcliffe's personal wealth will be vast. However, his retained interest in INEOS qualifies him for business property relief when he eventually passes away.

There is a huge justification in this, because INEOS reportedly employs thousands of people and contractors in the UK alone. If that business had to be broken up on Ratcliffe's death, it would be disruptive and injurious to the British economy.

I offer INEOS as an example of why any client that runs a business – irrespective of its scale, turnover and reach – should think seriously about the implications of the advantages of applying business property relief to their IHT Estate. This is not simply a matter of attempting to pay less in death duties; it's a social imperative that extends beyond the reach of someone's inner circle of family and loved ones.

---

13 INEOS, www.ineos.com/about/history, accessed 23 March 2023
14 INEOS, www.ineos.com/about, accessed 23 March 2023

Pensions

No matter the colour or flavour of the UK government holding power at any one time, each actively urges the workers of this country to set money aside for their retirement. Essentially, we're encouraged to accumulate money outside of our personal Estates during our working lives so that, by the time we retire, we can draw down on that pool of money, which then supplements whatever rate is offered by the State pension. The State-sponsored incentive to contribute to a private pension is intended to meet the social purpose of retirees continuing to enjoy a reasonably high standard of living, similar to the standard they became accustomed to during their working lives.

There are essentially two types of pensions:

1. Defined benefit pension (or occupational pension)
2. Defined contribution pension schemes

1. Defined benefit pension (or occupational pension)

This undertakes to meet the promise made by employers to provide employees with an income in retirement via a pension fund that invests money and builds up reserves.

Anyone who has an interest in an occupational fund exchanges their share of the value of those assets in return for a guaranteed pension for the rest of their lifetime. If their life is short, that provides a return to the pension fund, but if their life is long, the pension fund has a greater liability.

2. Defined contribution pension schemes

These are also known by various other names, including workplace pensions, personal pension plans and self-invested personal pensions (SIPPs).

The main difference with defined contribution pension schemes is that the pension received is entirely dependent on the money that sits within the pensioner's account.

The potential risk is that, over time, that pension pot becomes depleted and will eventually run out of money, leaving the pensioner to fall back entirely on the State pension provision and possibly any personal savings.

The other possibility with any defined contribution pension is that the pension fund may provide more money than is actually needed so that a surviving spouse, civil partner or other beneficiaries might receive a lump sum or, alternatively, a pension themselves. A SIPP falls outside the scope of IHT; instead, it is subject to its own taxation regime. An individual can decide who will inherit their SIPP, and this doesn't need to be restricted to family members – it can extend to friends or charities or be divided between a variety of beneficiaries.

The tax rules for defined contribution pension funds, including SIPPs, mean that it is possible to pass your pension pot on to your beneficiaries without any IHT liability due. For example, should the pensioner die before reaching the age of seventy-five, and the funds are transferred within two years following their death, then no IHT is due. However, it's worth noting that, should the beneficiaries elect to take the benefit as a lump sum without claiming it within two years, this will then attract income tax. No IHT is due with a death after the age of seventy-five, but income tax will be payable at their marginal tax rate by your beneficiaries on any amounts drawn from your pension scheme.

Gifts between husband and wife and civil partners

The area of gifts between husband and wife and civil partners also forms a category of social purpose. Before 1975, when a spouse died, death duties were payable on their entire Estate, despite the fact they may have left that Estate in their Will to their surviving spouse. Quite rightly, this was a shocking state of affairs and ruined many people's lives, adding untold hardship and misery on top of their grief for their loved ones.

When the law changed in 1975, it allowed for what is known as the 'surviving spouse exemption', which these days also applies to the surviving civil partner. The major change was that the surviving spouse or partner can now inherit the Estate of the deceased without any IHT liabilities. That applies if they inherit the Estate outright, or if they inherit what is left to them in a life interest trust fund, which is known as immediate post-death interest (IPDI).

> **CASE STUDY: The last laugh**
>
> One of my favourite stories concerns the late comedian Ken Dodd, himself no fan of HMRC (then known as the Inland Revenue) after they initiated legal proceedings against him for evading £800,000 of tax under the criminal code, having first pursued him under the civil code for the tax he owed.
>
> Following a three-week trial in Liverpool, Ken Dodd emerged victorious, but his wounds remained deep.
>
> Two days before his death, he married long-term partner Anne Jones, with whom he had shared his Liverpool home for the previous forty years. Had they not married, his Estate would have been liable for IHT to the sum of £2.6 million (against his estimated £7.2 million wealth).[15]

---

15 G Owen, 'Doddy gets the last laugh at the taxman', *Today's Wills & Probate* (2018), https://todayswillsandprobate.co.uk/ken-dodd-gets-last-laugh-taxman, accessed 27 March 2023

Dodd's action illustrates that assets can be passed between married couples free of IHT on death. More important than the money aspect, his story highlights the injustice in that the law discriminates between the ways in which a common-law partner, a married partner or a civil partner is treated in respect of IHT.

The surviving spouse may inherit the entire Estate tax-free, and they can also inherit any unused portion of the nil-rate band and the residence nil-rate band for when they die and their Estate is then subject to IHT. The nil-rate band (NRB) – also known as the IHT threshold – is the amount up to which no IHT is due. The residence nil-rate band (RNRB), introduced in 2017, is an additional allowance for reducing IHT when someone passes on their main residence in their Will, subject to certain conditions.

The benefits of NRB and RNRB do not apply to the common-law partner. With the judicious timing of his marriage, Dodd had the last laugh, as his supporters claimed, against HMRC.

7
The Impact Of Life Assurance

Life assurance is the great saviour for those many individuals for whom it's not possible, because of the size of their Estate or because of the class of assets owned, to avoid IHT on their Estate by lifetime giving. Insuring against the IHT liability on your death can solve this issue, either partially or entirely, simply by you paying a monthly, annual or single premium.

Although many people I meet set out with good intentions in respect of their life assurance policy, not all of them see the policy to term, instead allowing it to lapse by the time they die. There are numerous reasons why this happens. Principally, it is because they find the premium becomes too expensive, particularly (and ironically) with what is called low-cost life assurance. Often people don't realise that most policies are flexible, which allows them to abandon part of their cover so they can continue to pay an affordable premium. The consequence of abandoning the policy in its entirety is self-evident, in that the insurance company will no longer have any liability to make a payment at the time when it's needed most.

In this chapter, I will outline some of the general principles behind what life assurance can provide, which, in turn, may help you decide on a course of action you have not previously fully considered. It's a means whereby you can be reassured that your heirs may not need to draw down from your Estate directly to pay the death duties owed to the government. In that sense, this chapter will answer in a direct way the central premise of this book, 'Who will get my money when I die?', to which the response should be, 'Not HMRC'.

The benefits of life assurance

I often find that clients don't always consider life assurance as a way of paying an IHT liability. This is despite it being a viable option, for the following two reasons:

1. The proceeds from the life assurance can be held outside of your own Estate for IHT and thus attract no liability if the life policy is properly structured.

THE IMPACT OF LIFE ASSURANCE

2. The sooner you start to hold life assurance for a meaningful amount while in the prime of life, the cost of the premium is much reduced compared with taking out a policy later in life. For example, you may choose to pay a flat-rate premium for the life of the contract, whereby the amount paid in the first month remains the same until the policy pays out.

In general, life policies typically offer two benefits:

1. Any investment element to the life policy attracts a redemption value, which you can cash in for yourself.

2. Death benefit is only paid out when you die, but you can assign this to a family trust fund, which can be held on terms that are similar to the terms of your Will and can be used to pay any IHT due.

Irrespective of the size of an Estate, broadly speaking, the premium for every pound covered is the same. This is regardless of the size of the policy, although some discounts are available for particularly large policies. However, it's worth noting that the marketplace does limit its risk exposure in relation to a single person, and so it goes without saying that it's much easier to obtain cover for £5 million than for £50 million.

Knowing the level at which to set the required cover is key to the whole process. In the first instance, it's necessary to quantify the IHT, and only then can an individual realistically propose the level of cover that is appropriate to them. For particularly large amounts of cover, the terms offered by the life assurance company would necessarily be bespoke, based on a number of factors, from age to health conditions. For an amount that the market considers to be more 'normal', there are rarely any difficulties in obtaining the level of cover requested.

I highly recommend life assurance to everyone who is looking to maximise the benefits offered by planning for their IHT liability. As a cog in the planning wheel, I describe life assurance as 'the great saviour' because it can – and frequently does – avoid any of the IHT injustices I have described and witness regularly. An example is the unmarried couple with children, where the one partner dies, leaving their wealth to their unmarried partner but not without a punitive IHT liability due. Certainly, marriage isn't for everyone, and remaining unmarried is a perfectly legitimate choice. However, a life assurance policy can protect against that unwelcome IHT expense and protect the future lifestyle of those that are loved and left behind.

Obtaining life assurance is easier than ever today and can be arranged by simply answering a set of questions online in return for a quoted price. Alternatively, to insure larger sums, you can engage a broker to help achieve the best possible terms for your circumstances, including your state of health. As a secondary consideration, if you are thinking of assigning the death benefit payout to a trust, I advise engaging the services of solicitors rather than opting for the standard trust terms provided by retail life assurance companies.

Understanding your choices

There are four main categories of life assurance:

1. Level premium assurance
2. Single premium life assurance
3. Low-cost life assurance
4. Term assurance

These types of policies can be written either on a single life basis or a joint lives basis, depending on when the IHT liability is expected to arise, for example, on the death of the survivor of a married couple or a civil partnership.

1. Level premium assurance

Once terms have been agreed with a provider, level premium assurance requires a monthly or annual premium to be paid at the same guaranteed amount for the remainder of your lifetime until you die, which is when the death benefit of the life policy pays out.

When this sum isn't aggregated with your IHT Estate, the payment is typically to the family trust fund. For many people, this is the simplest and most effective policy to organise and protect their wealth against IHT liabilities at a time when family and loved ones will most need protection and reassurance.

2. Single premium life assurance

This is similar to level premium assurance, except that a lump sum is payable to the insurance company on the first day that cover commences.

The cover then exists, with no further premiums due, for the remainder of your life. The benefits upon death are the same as with level premium cover.

3. Low-cost life assurance

Premiums are based on a person's state of health at the point the policy is taken and are guaranteed only for ten years (or exceptionally, as such term is agreed). When the term ends, the premium is then repriced. However, it's important to note that the premium isn't repriced based on your then health but rather beneficially on your health at the time the life policy was originally taken.

While the new premium will be based on current market conditions, variables will be taken into consideration. These will include the consideration that you are now ten years older, and the closer you get to the end of your life – actuarially speaking, of course – typically the premium on a low-cost life insurance policy increases significantly.

4. Term assurance

This is ideal cover for anyone looking to mirror their IHT liability. It's a short-term arrangement designed to protect against the recipients of lifetime gifts having to pay IHT should the donor die within seven years from the day they made the gift.

Term assurance is good at protecting against the IHT liability that would arise on a failed potentially exempt transfer. In addition, the IHT liability can reduce during this seven-year period because of taper relief. For example, the IHT liability reduces by 20% for every year after the third year the donor remains alive since the date of the gift. Assuming the donor does not die in that seven-year period, the IHT is reduced to a nil liability, and the life cover also falls away as it is no longer needed. See Chapter 8 for further details on taper relief.

Risks

I mentioned above that some people choose to discontinue their life assurance premiums, principally on grounds of cost and their need to save money. The impact of choosing not to continue with policies is usually highlighted when those heavy death duties become due. Without an underwritten life policy that will help pay towards them, it usually becomes apparent that the monthly premium was indeed the more affordable option.

It pains me to see parents who can't afford life assurance premiums sacrificing their children's inheritance as a result. However, all might not be lost; rather than cancelling the policy and losing the benefit of the cover, there are options available whereby their (adult) children can undertake to pay the premium, particularly if the offspring are doing well in their own lives and careers.

It could otherwise be that, in earlier times, the children already benefited from lifetime giving from their parents, in the form of assets or even cash. Just because the parents may not now be cash-rich but are wealthy on paper (such as with properties or other illiquid assets) shouldn't necessarily result in a false economy by saving on paying life assurance premiums.

If, for example, the children have been gifted properties that accrue a rental income that was once collected by the parents, they will have already benefited from the proceeds of their parents' generosity. It is therefore not such a burden for the children to adopt paying for the insurance premiums, especially if they will in this way mitigate the IHT liabilities on their parents' remaining assets.

This is a scenario I encounter surprisingly often. I attribute that to people not knowing what it is they actually own and therefore having no clear picture of the future ramifications of cancelling insurance.

Planning to avoid failure

Of course, people's wealth – be that in cash, assets, equities and/or properties – can fluctuate over time, which is perhaps one reason why people are unsure as to what their accumulated wealth really amounts to. If you're considering taking out a life assurance policy, this is a good time to begin an evaluation process and to bring your wealth into sharper focus. You need to bear in mind that when you do take a life assurance policy, you will only be covered to the extent of your declared liability.

Given that your wealth position may change, it's possible to build indexing into the level of cover, on the assumption that your asset values will increase over time. Indexing your cover has a distinct advantage such as when your circumstances change. That may be from owning investment assets to owning agricultural or business assets (which attract 100% IHT relief).

Alternatively, you might engage in lifetime giving, so much so that assets cease to be part of your Estate. In such cases, when you die and the insurance payout is collected, there is a possibility that the amount received from the life assurance company will exceed the final IHT liability. This leads to a legitimate surplus for the family, although it should be remembered that life companies will only insure liabilities calculated at the time of taking a policy. I like to think of that as a happy coincidence.

Conversely, should the family asset values significantly increase beyond the value calculated at the time of taking the life policy, the policy could result in the Estate being underinsured. In this case, it's always worthwhile seeking professional advice to see if you need to consider indexing to be a part of the life assurance decision process, or whether further cover should be taken as the value of your Estate increases.

My best advice will always be, whenever possible, to start the life assurance process when you are young. The premiums will be much lower than if you decide to think about this in your middle age or beyond.

No matter which route is taken, it is always worthwhile reviewing the decisions periodically to take into account your state of health and the change in your wealth.

8
Making Lifetime Gifts And Surviving Seven Years

Making gifts in your lifetime is one of the best ways of determining before you die who will get your money. It can also be an effective way of reducing your IHT liability.

For IHT purposes, gifts can be categorised as those that are:

- Exempt from IHT
- Potentially exempt from IHT
- Chargeable to IHT at the lifetime tax rate

Each category is examined separately after the position between spouses and civil partners has been considered.

It may surprise you to learn that there are no limits to how much you can give away through lifetime giving. At first, even thinking about giving money away to family in our own lifetimes does strike many as oddly counterintuitive. Most people I talk to about this at first take the view as a fait accompli that their accumulated wealth will only pass down at the end of their natural lifetime.

Those who realise what that might mean to their Estate in respect of IHT liabilities begin to see that the aim of making a lifetime gift essentially sets their successors up for their lifetime. When that translates into one generation giving substantial sums to the next, I've noticed that those in the recipient generation consider this more as holding the money in trust for the next generation rather than as a resource to be consumed. It evolves into an appreciation that each generation can enjoy the benefit of that money during their lifetime, in the knowledge that that they are looking after it and growing it before passing it on themselves. Family wealth thus takes on a greater value beyond its monetary worth, and those families with a dynastic legacy to preserve – for example, where there's a family business, farm or even a stately home – pass on their wealth through the generations with the purpose of retaining that asset.

Even a modest gift can have a distinct purpose in mind, such as paying off a mortgage or funding school fees for grandchildren. No matter what the purpose of the gift, however large or small it is, and whether it is in cash or any other assets you own, the net results remain the same – a reduction in the IHT liabilities, and the ability to control who gets your money when you die.

The point of lifetime giving is that it's not a deathbed wish. Where required, as long as the donor survives seven years, that gift is exempt from IHT liability. If the donor dies within those seven years, the gift is then subject to taper relief, as covered later in this chapter. Alternatively, the gift may be exempt or may attract 100% relief as business or agricultural property.

Typically, people consider lifetime giving as they progress through their late fifties and early sixties, and certainly by the time they're into their seventies. Much older than that, and it's looking less likely that lifetime giving will be considered, as the donor may not survive the seven years to make the gift exempt from IHT.

Making lifetime gifts is one course of action that epitomises the voluntary aspect of IHT, thanks to the seven-year-rule exemption. The circumstances outlined in this chapter, which could persuade you to contemplate lifetime giving, might be especially compelling if you are concerned about IHT liability when you die and what will remain in your Estate to be passed on to your heirs. You might also be persuaded if you're confident your wealth exceeds what you will probably need to see you through to the end of your natural lifetime, and that you will realistically survive seven years after making a lifetime gift.

With this in mind, the following will outline how IHT treats and categorises those gifts.

Gifts that are exempt from IHT

The following lifetime gifts are always exempt:

- Gifts to your spouse or civil partner
- Gifts of up to £250 to different individuals
- Donations to qualifying charities or political groups
- Gifts as normal expenditure from income
- Wedding gifts (£5,000 from a parent, £2,500 from a grandparent, £1,000 from others)

Not all the rules and exemptions are simple, as you would expect, so the following explains the main details you need to be aware of.

Gifts between husband and wife or civil partners

These are exempt from IHT both in respect of lifetime gifts and gifts made on death. The exemption is unlimited in value, and no Capital Gains Tax is due on the gift but the donee will inherit the donor's CGT base cost which will apply on a subsequent disposal. The surviving spouse or civil partner can also benefit from any money held in a trust fund from which they benefit.

Annual exemption

The annual exemption for IHT is £3,000 for any gifts in any tax year. Any portion of that annual exemption not used in a tax year may be carried forward for one tax year only.

The exemption can be used against a larger gift. When several gifts are made in the same tax year, the annual exemption is given against the earlier gifts. However, if several gifts are made on the same day, the annual exemption is allocated pro rata to the gifts, regardless of the order made.

If exempt but potentially chargeable and immediately chargeable lifetime transfers are all being made in one tax year, the immediately chargeable lifetime transfer should be made first so that the annual exemption is not wasted.

Small gifts exemption

Outright gifts of up to £250 to any number of persons are exempt from tax. This exemption cannot be used in conjunction with another exemption on the same gift.

Gifts in contemplation of marriage or formation of a civil partnership

Gifts made in contemplation of a marriage or civil partnership are exempt, at least up to specific amounts.

The exemption varies depending on the relationship between the donor and donee. Gifts are exempt up to £1,000 per recipient, increasing to £2,500 for a grandchild or great-grandchild, and £5,000 for a child. This exemption is in addition to the annual exemption.

Normal expenditure out of income exemption

This can be potentially significant. A person who enjoys an especially high income but has relatively low living expenses can give away all of their excess income, which is then exempt from the date of gift rather than being subject to the seven-year rule, on the proviso that the donor is left with enough income to maintain their usual standard of living.

This is an extremely useful exemption because the donor doesn't need to survive the seven years required for a potentially exempt transfer, as discussed below. As a consequence, significant sums of money can potentially be gifted each year, taking advantage of this exemption. It's often used to make transfers into a trust, thus avoiding a hefty IHT charge, either on chargeable lifetime transfers or on transfers arising on death.

The three conditions for normal expenditure out of income exemption are:

1. The expenditure is part of the normal expenditure of the donor.

2. The expenditure is made out of the income of the donor, taking one year with another – ie even if the donor's income and expenditure vary, they can still afford to make gifts to others.

3. The donor is left with sufficient income to maintain their usual standard of living.

Determining the income of the donor is usually straightforward, as it is verifiable against their tax returns. Likewise, determining the donor's expenditure is also straightforward via reference to their bank account, although whether it is considered part of the normal expenditure requires more careful consideration. For example, is there an expenditure pattern, and did the donor comply with their commitment to making specific payments? HMRC indicates that a settled pattern spanning three to four years is normal to demonstrate the required pattern, although a single gift may meet this test if it is considered the first in a pattern of gifts. Documenting the intention is advisable.

As to the gifts themselves, it's recognised that the pattern of giving can be complex, but that gifts made for a special purpose should be disregarded.

Conditional exemption for heritage property

In some circumstances, buildings, land, works of art and other objects can be exempt from IHT when they are passed on, either as the result of a death or as a gift. This has the effect of deferring the charge to IHT and, where the conditions are observed, there is no IHT liability.

There are three categories for assets granted conditional exemption for heritage property:

1. Pre-eminent buildings or land of national, historic, scientific or artistic interest
2. Land of outstanding scenic, historic or scientific interest
3. Buildings of outstanding or architectural interest, and the amenity land and chattels historically associated with such buildings

The new owner is obliged to make an agreement, known as 'the undertakings', to:

- Look after the item
- Make it available for the general public to view
- Keep it within the UK

If the conditions are broken by the new owner, the IHT charge is restored, the exemption is withdrawn and the IHT must be paid.

> **CASE STUDY: Gifts to the Nation**
>
> Each year, it is announced that certain works of art have been accepted in lieu of IHT. In 2021, items worth £52 million were allocated to museums across the UK by Arts Council England.[16] These included Sir Anthony van Dyck's *Portrait of a Woman*, John Turner's *Walton Bridge* and LS Lowry's painting of David Lloyd George's birthplace in Manchester.

Death while on active service or working for the emergency services

IHT is not charged on the death of an individual from a wound inflicted, or as a result of contracting a disease, while a member of the armed forces and on active service. The injury or disease does not need to be the major contributory cause of death, and the passage of time is not in itself a bar to the exemption. This relief also extends to emergency service personnel, including police officers.

Gifts to charities and national institutions

You can leave your assets to charities, museums, galleries, government departments, local authorities

---

16 N Khomami, 'Works by Turner and Lowry donated to British nation in 2021', *The Guardian* (2021), www.theguardian.com/culture/2021/dec/10/turner-lowry-gifted-uk-nation-2021-arts-council-england, accessed 29 November 2023

and universities. Typically, a collector or artist will bequeath a significant body of work that has been accumulated in their lifetime, and this will be exempt from IHT.

Potentially exempt transfers (PETs) for IHT

All gifts between individuals are PETs, other than those between spouses or civil partners. A PET is treated as an exempt transfer while the donor is alive, meaning that PETs will not give rise to a lifetime IHT charge.

PETs are arguably one of the most significant opportunities to reduce your liability to IHT. There are other forms of PETs, in addition to gifts, concerning transfers to and from trust funds. These are discussed in Chapter 9.

A PET becomes an exempt transfer if the donor survives for seven years from the date of the gift. If the donor dies within seven years, an IHT charge will arise and tax will be payable by the donee.

Taper relief reduces the tax payable where gifts are made between four to seven years before the donor's death. The tapering is applied to the tax payable on a sliding scale, as shown in the following table.

MAKING LIFETIME GIFTS AND SURVIVING SEVEN YEARS

IHT taper relief on gifts within seven years of death

Years between gift and date of death	Percentage of death charge	Effective IHT tax rate
Fewer than three	100%	40%
Three to four	80%	32%
Four to five	60%	24%
Five to six	40%	16%
Six to seven	20%	8%
Seven or more	0%	0%

Example

A parent, who has made no other gifts in their lifetime, gives their child £1 million in cash.

The parent dies between five and six years from the date of the gift.

The IHT due on the gift is as follows:

Failed PET	£1,000,000
Less nil-rate band	(£325,000)
Chargeable gift	£675,000
IHT @ 40%	**£270,000**
Taper relief	(£162,000)
IHT payable	£108,000

The PET in this example is then known as a failed PET, and the amount of the gift is brought into the value of the donor's Estate for IHT purposes.

Failed PETs can still be considered advantageous, as the value of the gift is frozen at the date of the gift. Any increase in value from the date of gift to the date of death escapes a charge to IHT on the death of the donor. Furthermore, if the value of a failed PET has fallen from the date of the gift to the date of death, it is the reduced value that is brought back into charge in the donor's Estate at the date of death.

Gifts chargeable to IHT at the lifetime tax rate

Lifetime chargeable gifts that do not qualify as PETs are – as the name suggests – immediately chargeable to IHT at the lifetime tax rate. The main category of chargeable transfers at the lifetime tax rate is where individuals put money into a family trust fund, where the trust fund is usually held on discretionary terms. In those circumstances, IHT is payable at half the normal rate payable on death.

If the donor dies within the seven years, the amount of the gift is brought into the value of the donor's Estate for IHT purposes, but the amount of the IHT liability on the lifetime gift is reduced by taper relief and the IHT already paid during lifetime, subject to the credit not exceeding the IHT liability on death. If, however, the donor survives seven years from the date of the gift, there is no further IHT due.

There are also complications when there are both lifetime chargeable gifts and failed PETs. The order in which the gifts are made can adversely affect the amount of IHT payable. Generally, due to the way the calculation works, the PET should be made before the chargeable lifetime transfer.

To gift or not to gift?

There are some limited circumstances when a gift is not regarded as a gift for IHT purposes:

1. Bad bargains
2. Gifts for family maintenance

1. Bad bargains

If it can be shown that no gratuitous benefit was intended, there is no IHT charge. Essentially, this is intended to make commercial transactions exempt from IHT. It will be necessary to show that a sale made at an undervalue to a family member was the sort of transaction that might have been made with an unconnected third party, for example because money was needed urgently.

2. Gifts for family maintenance

These can include gifts to benefit parties to a marriage or civil partnership, legitimate and illegitimate children, and dependent relatives.

Whenever you make a gift, always keep a clear and transparent record that can be easily found with your paperwork when needed to verify your actions. In my experience, when a new client approaches me for advice on how to plan their Will, they're not necessarily thinking 'What can I do to reduce my IHT liability when I die?'. Instead, they are wondering what will happen to their money when they die and what they can do to improve the potential outcomes of that. My starting point is very much making sure that, if they are contemplating giving money away in their lifetime, it's not to the detriment of their remaining lifetime. They must ensure they retain sufficient money to meet their own needs, no matter what those needs are. It's all a matter of context, but the primary objective is normally for them to avoid becoming dependent on others.

Some people approach the subject of lifetime giving by prioritising IHT liability reduction over their own needs. However, when we explore the options I've outlined above, my clients can usually strike a better balance. I would argue that looking after yourself is always of higher importance, and the Kaiser Family

Foundation research mentioned in Chapter 1 suggests this is true for many individuals.[17] As we get older, our priorities change in respect of our own mental and physical wellbeing, and that isn't something any of us should consider as being selfish. We all want our needs to be catered for as we grow older, so it's not a sensible option to give everything we have away simply to avoid paying tax when we die. Similarly, it is sensible to make sure that following any gifts, you don't need to ask your children to support you financially. Living is not just about giving others joy through gifting – it's also about enjoying your own life.

How much money you should or shouldn't give away centres on first calculating what your IHT liability will be, followed by asking the questions:

- How can I change the assets I own?
- What can I own that is free of IHT liability?
- Is some of my wealth held in financial structures which are outside the scope of IHT?
- Can I arrange life assurance as an alternative to relying on lifetime giving?

---

17 L Hamel, B Wu and M Brodie, *Views and Experiences with End-of-Life Medical Care in the U.S.* (KFF, 2017), https://files.kff.org/attachment/Report-Views-and-Experiences-with-End-of-Life-Medical-Care-in-the-US, accessed 24 March 2023

WHO WILL GET MY MONEY WHEN I DIE?

Once you have gained perspective from these questions, you can afford to make decisions on whether you, your loved ones and your Estate will benefit most from your lifetime gifts, assuming you survive for seven years after making them.

9
Putting Assets Into Trust For Future Generations

In this chapter, I will explain the taxation status relating to trusts, and also why trusts are one of the most enduring concepts for holding private wealth in a common-law jurisdiction such as England and Wales.

The law of trusts first came into being way back in the annals of English history, from the time of the crusades in the twelfth century. Whenever a member of the landed gentry left England's shores to fight for king and country, he conveyed ownership of his Estate to be managed in his absence by people he trusted. This was done on the basis that, on his return, the ownership of his Estate would be conveyed back to him. The concept of trust had been born, later leading to the terms 'beneficiary' and 'trustee'.

Today anyone can create a trust fund at any financial threshold through the use of a document known as a trust deed, which is drawn up by a lawyer. The two considerations that most often play a role in the formation of trust deeds are maintaining the family dynamic, and the consequences of taxation upon the death of the benefactor.

The family dynamic is usually the most important consideration in setting up a trust. Considerations include parents who are concerned about the impact of leaving large sums to their children or grandchildren, whom they might feel need to be more financially mature before gaining direct access to the funds. Or a parent may be concerned about the longevity of a relationship their adult child or grandchild is involved in.

Many of my clients draw up their Will at a time when their children are simply too young for the parents to form a complete view as to what their children's futures hold. This is particularly relevant when a child has a disability and lacks the capacities to manage their own affairs, and will need trustees to act in their interest for the remainder of their natural life.

Taxation is therefore not the primary consideration in setting up a trust in these circumstances. It's more important to these people to ringfence and protect their children or grandchildren's development and future wellbeing, which sometimes extends beyond reaching adulthood. Establishing a trust with its own conditions of access to funds and, where appropriate, a Letter of Wishes to guide the trustees in relation to how they may act in certain circumstances, satisfies these concerns.

Where there is a dynastic trust fund, a Letter of Wishes may offer guidance to when the funds should be passed on to the subsequent generation (such as to the grandchildren rather than the children). The Letter of Wishes may give guidance about how the private wealth held in trust could be managed. Alternatively, it might offer guidance stating that, when the children reach a certain age, in all probability they won't need the protection of a trust fund. Consideration should be given at that point to granting the children some capital outright, or in some cases to winding up the trust and bringing it to an end, or giving the children control of the trust fund.

CASE STUDY: When a Duke attempted to disinherit his heir

In some circumstances, the family dynamic and associated legacy is considered to be in the UK national interest. Such was the case with the Blenheim Estate, where the resultant trust was established by an act of Parliament in 1705, holding the Estate for the Dukes of Marlborough in succession.[18]

---

18 S Panesar, *Equity and Trusts* (Pearson, 2020)

> Although this might seem archaic, with little or no relevance to today, only as recently as 1994 was the law tested in respect of the conditions set down by the trust.
>
> The case centred on the then eleventh Duke of Marlborough attempting to restrict his son's interest in the Blenheim Estate. His son, Jamie Blandford, then had a seemingly inappropriate lifestyle. The eleventh Duke seemed to have been greatly concerned that the thriving Estate business he had worked so hard to build would fall apart with his son at its helm.
>
> The ensuing court case was bitterly fought, and the Duke was successful in placing the Estate under the control of the trustees rather than Jamie, who was then on probation for theft and forgery. Upon the eleventh Duke's death in October 2014, Jamie inherited the title, becoming the twelfth Duke, and the Estate passed to trustees in a sign of good financial and taxation planning.
>
> Thankfully, a significant rapprochement occurred between father and son before the eleventh Duke passed away.

The great advantage of discretionary trusts

In general, those families who set up discretionary trusts tend to retain and grow their wealth more successfully. There are two known reasons for this:

1. The trustees can determine how much each beneficiary receives each year. If there is undistributed income, it can be retained or accumulated, and if capital gains are realised, they accrue to the trust fund itself.

2. There is a different and predictable IHT regime applying to discretionary trusts (and, since 2006, other types of trusts), where the charge to IHT occurs at a rate of up to 6% every ten years. This is instead of the 40% IHT charge on the death of a wealth-holding member of the family, the timing of which is usually unpredictable.

Once inside the structure of a discretionary trust, wealth is no longer regarded – for IHT purposes – as part of an individual's personal Estate. This solves a huge problem for people who hold significant wealth. Discretionary trusts offer a clear idea as to how much IHT will be payable, because it is up to 6% of the wealth held in trust. They also give accuracy as to when the charge is payable – namely, every ten years – and the charge is not determined by a death. Discretionary trusts are therefore not only predictable, but they are also a safety net. They allow people to save up for the trusts or to accumulate income that allows them to manage the payment of IHT, as opposed to an individual's Estate receiving an unwelcome and large IHT liability after they have died.

Discretionary trusts also deal with some of the unfortunate circumstances that can arise.

Example

A grandfather dies at the age of ninety, having been predeceased by his wife, resulting in IHT being payable. The residue of his Estate is left to his son.

If the son dies in the years immediately following his father's passing, IHT is once again payable on the son's death. This means that the Estate has, in reality, been doubly taxed. This is unless the Estate is subject to quick succession relief, which is applicable only within the five-year period after the first death. Quick succession relief is where credit is given against the IHT due on the second death for the IHT paid on the first death, albeit tapered over the five years following the first death.

Different types of trusts and settlements

It is important to understand that any trust or settlement generally falls into one of two categories:

1. Discretionary trusts

2. Life interest trusts

The IHT regime for trusts and settlements changed significantly on 22 March 2006. Prior to this, there were effectively two different regimes: one for trusts where the beneficiaries had a life interest; and one where there was no life interest – in other words, a discretionary trust.

In most cases it's clear whether or not a life interest exists. A beneficiary who has an immediate right to receive income, or to use and enjoy trust property, normally has a life interest. Where there is no life interest, the trust is normally regarded as a discretionary trust, since the trustees can distribute the trust income at their discretion between the beneficiaries or, alternatively, can accumulate the undistributed income to increase the capital value of the trust fund.

In broad terms, my belief is that the reason for the change was to ensure a higher amount of IHT was paid under the 40% regime from 22 March 2006 onwards, and to discourage people from using trusts as a means of growing and preserving wealth. The new rules therefore contribute to the 'law of unintended consequences', whereby people's behaviour changes so that they retain more money in their own names. In effect, they therefore pay more IHT when they die, or they gift money away during their lifetime.

The law of unintended consequences results in situations when people's judgement can become clouded and their money, after they die, ends up not being held in the most appropriate manner. Did they really mean to gift money to the spendthrift child? Did they really intend for their child, who is in an unsatisfactory relationship, to inherit everything and put the family wealth at risk? Did they really want their Estate to be aggregated with the financial resources considered on divorce? These are questions I often ask clients who have not received full and complete advice in respect of their long-term decision making.

In practical terms, the main effect of the 2006 changes is that all trust funds created on or after 22 March 2006 are within the ten-year charge, also known as the 6% regime. Creating trust funds in lifetime or on death without an immediate payment of IHT is now limited to:

- Gifts into trust up to the amount of the nil-rate band of the donor. This can be enhanced by both husband and wife (or civil partner) utilising their available nil-rate bands with gifts between them, since these are exempt under the spouse exemption. This can also be repeated every seven years, as the previous gift falls out of account for IHT purposes.

- Gifts into trust of property that attract 100% relief under either agricultural property relief or business property relief and where no IHT is payable on the transfer into trust, regardless of the value of the assets being transferred.

- Gifts into trust where the amount transferred falls within the normal expenditure out of income exemption. Again, the amount of the relief is limited only by the individual's income in excess of their normal expenditure for maintaining their usual standard of living.

- Gifts into a bare trust, where the trustee holds the legal title to the property, but the beneficiary holds the beneficial interest. Bare trusts are not settled property for IHT purposes.

Since, under the legislation introduced in 2006, the type of the trust no longer affects the IHT treatment for newly created trusts, they may now be created with non-tax considerations in mind. The options have been distilled into the following:

- To select a discretionary trust for the maximum flexibility in distributing funds within a class of beneficiaries

- To limit the class of beneficiaries more narrowly, to achieve a purpose such as funding education and initial property purchase for grandchildren

- To give an individual an old-style life interest trust so they are entitled to an income from the trust in circumstances where the trust fund's value isn't aggregated with their personal Estate for IHT purposes and so escapes an IHT charge on their death

- As the above point, but where the trustees can remove the right to income and bestow it on another beneficiary without IHT consequences

How IHT applies under the 6% regime

There are three occasions when a trust under the 6% regime may incur an IHT liability:

1. Creation
2. Every tenth anniversary
3. Exit

Although referred to as the 6% regime, often the IHT due will be less than 6%, as a result of the way the charge is calculated.

1. Creation

The amount of IHT payable depends on whether the trust fund is created during lifetime or on death.

Lifetime

For a lifetime transfer, there is an immediate charge to IHT at half the rates applying on death. The amount chargeable to IHT is calculated in the usual way, using the normal valuation principles and taking into account any available agricultural property relief or business property relief. The amount of IHT payable is then calculated at 0% on the portion within the settlor's nil-rate band available, and thereafter at 20%.

Example

George and his wife Lilian want to establish a discretionary trust for the benefit of their children and grandchildren. They have not made any previous lifetime transfers. None of the property being transferred is either agricultural or business property.

George and Lilian can each transfer into the trust fund an amount equal to the nil-rate band, currently £325,000; and two annual exemptions, at £3,000 each, or £6,000 in total, if those annual exemptions have not been used. The total amount transferred into the trust fund is therefore £662,000 with no IHT payable.

After seven years, the full nil-rate band is restored to them, meaning they can create a further trust fund with two nil-rate bands and, if available, two additional annual exemptions.

If the donor dies within seven years of the transfer to the trust fund, there may be a further IHT charge. This applies if the IHT paid already on the lifetime transfer is less than the IHT calculated as payable on the death of the settlor.

Death

The IHT is calculated in the normal way on the deceased's Estate and is payable from the Estate itself. Thereafter, the property passes to the trustees of the trust fund.

2. Tenth anniversary

The tenth anniversary charge attracts a charge to IHT at the maximum rate of 6%, although, with careful planning, that rate can be reduced. In particular, it will always be beneficial for the donor to transfer property into a trust fund when they have no chargeable transfers within the previous seven years. The same applies if there are no related settlements, namely ones created on the same day.

3. Exit

When trustees make a capital distribution, ie transfer assets such as money or buildings, from a trust to a beneficiary, there is a charge to IHT at a proportionate rate of up to 6%. The rate of charge is a proportion of the rate charged on the previous 10-year anniversary and is one-fortieth of the number of complete quarters that have elapsed since the previous anniversary.

For example, if the IHT rate on the previous anniversary was 5%, and a capital distribution was made in the twenty-fifth quarter, the rate of charge would be 3%, being twenty-four quarters out of forty quarters, multiplied by the previous 5% rate.

Trusts not in the 6% regime

Trusts not in the 6% regime arise when a beneficiary typically has a life interest that was created on or before 22 March 2006. Subsequent to this date, if a trust is created as an IPDI – an immediate post-death interest – it also falls outside of the 6% regime. IPDIs classically arise on the death of a spouse or civil partner, where the deceased's Estate is left in trust for their spouse or civil partner. During the life of an IPDI, no ten-year or exit charges are due.

Significantly, with trusts not in the 6% regime, the money within those trust funds is aggregated with the personal Estate of the beneficiary on their death. In other words, the surviving spouse or civil partner is treated in the same way as owning the assets personally, and the trustees will find themselves exposed to a significant IHT charge. This gives a persuasive argument for establishing trusts within the 6% regime, to avoid an increase to IHT liability.

The key point is that it must be a matter of good judgement to assess your IHT liability. In reality, for some people, a 40% IHT charge is quite acceptable if they also own a significant portfolio of property that then attracts 100% relief under agricultural property relief or business property relief. Alternatively, they may have quantified their IHT liability but hold the appropriate level of life insurance to offset against that expense.

Without doubt, the whole scenario of setting up trusts that are most appropriate for your Estate, family needs and future wishes can be a complex undertaking. I suggest it behoves anyone with any significant wealth or assets to seek complete advice from an experienced advisor who understands the minutiae of Estate planning. It is crucial to ensure that you don't delay in starting those conversations about what you really want to happen to your money when you die. It's also vital to possess an accurate assessment of your wealth and of your prospective IHT liability.

Knowing your IHT liability is essential, since it may impact on your plans for your money when you die, and potentially also in your lifetime. Only when you bring together all of these factors will you find yourself in a position to make those informed decisions – not only for you to live with, but to live on as testament to a life well lived.

PART THREE
BRING IT ALL TOGETHER

In the previous chapters, I have described the various options that will help you calculate your IHT liability and the measures that can be put in place to offset that charge.

I will now describe how you can structure your Estate tax efficiently in a way that ensures your wishes for who will inherit your money are carried out, while also allowing you to retain control of your wealth during your lifetime. This final part therefore brings everything together with the four building blocks of Estate planning:

1. Assessing your personal wealth
2. Lifetime giving

3. Structuring your Will

4. Death benefits

By adopting this approach, you can consider every aspect of your Estate as well as ensure your wishes are carried out. These building blocks can be considered either as discrete subjects or, alternatively, as a comprehensive, step-by-step method reflecting your individuality and how you wish to approach planning for your Estate.

Either way, it gives you a solid foundation from which to consider your financial affairs and to make arrangements for drafting your Will as a part of planning for your Estate. This should provide you with a great source of comfort, knowing that matters have been properly addressed.

10
The Four Building Blocks Of Estate Planning

In this chapter, I first describe the four building blocks of Estate planning. I then go into greater detail as to how they can work for you.

The four building blocks are:

1. **Assessing your personal wealth:** This first building block is where you need to consider the size of your personal wealth and make a proportionate plan. There is no point having the most sophisticated Estate plan if your wealth is consumed by the professional costs of implementing that plan. With larger amounts of personal wealth, a greater level of planning for your Estate may become appropriate.

2. **Lifetime giving:** The second building block is to consider what, if any, planning you should undertake in your lifetime. This can include giving money to or for the benefit of your family; or it could be to outside your family, for example to charitable causes. Individuals tend to first consider lifetime giving when approaching their late fifties or their early sixties. By the time of their late sixties and early seventies, if they have personal wealth in excess of their own needs, it is often being gifted to younger generations – children and sometimes grandchildren.

3. **Structuring your Will:** The third building block is to consider how to structure your Will. This may be straightforward where tax planning is the main concern. Alternatively, it may need to take into account special situations such as blended families or children with disabilities. How you structure your Will is key to making sure your wishes are carried out after you have died.

4. **Death benefits:** This final building block is where you will make arrangements for those financial benefits that arise only on your death – the death benefits on your pension schemes and the proceeds on any life assurance policy. These arrangements are made in your lifetime, but like your Will, sit in the background until you have died.

THE FOUR BUILDING BLOCKS OF ESTATE PLANNING

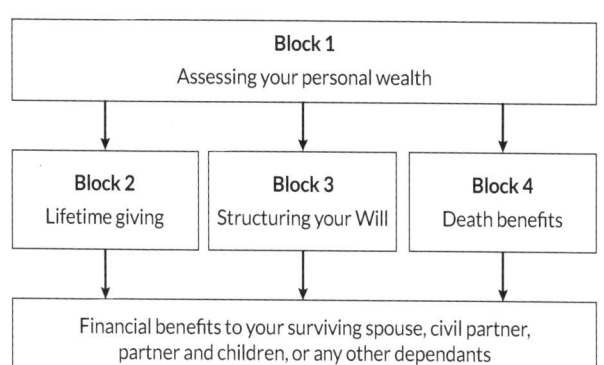

The four building blocks can be illustrated as follows:

```
┌─────────────────────────────────────────────┐
│                  Block 1                    │
│        Assessing your personal wealth       │
└─────────────────────────────────────────────┘
        │              │              │
        ▼              ▼              ▼
┌──────────────┐ ┌──────────────┐ ┌──────────────┐
│   Block 2    │ │   Block 3    │ │   Block 4    │
│Lifetime giving│ │Structuring   │ │Death benefits│
│              │ │your Will     │ │              │
└──────────────┘ └──────────────┘ └──────────────┘
        │              │              │
        ▼              ▼              ▼
┌─────────────────────────────────────────────┐
│ Financial benefits to your surviving spouse,│
│ civil partner, partner and children, or any │
│ other dependants                            │
└─────────────────────────────────────────────┘
```

The four building blocks of planning

Taken together, these four building blocks of planning provide a comprehensive approach to dealing with your Estate, to ensure your IHT liability is minimised and that your wishes for your wealth are carried out.

Building block 1: Assessing your personal wealth

In Chapter 3, I described the process you should follow to ascertain your personal wealth. This is a useful starting point as it helps determine how sophisticated the arrangements for your Estate need to be.

Once you have calculated your total wealth, either individually or as a couple, it helps then to categorise that total between:

WHO WILL GET MY MONEY WHEN I DIE?

1. The assets qualifying for business property relief or agricultural property relief, on which no IHT is payable

2. The remainder, on which IHT at 40% will ordinarily be payable

If IHT is payable on any part of your Estate, you need to consider your potential options, both to minimise the amount of IHT and to make sure your wishes for your Estate are carried out.

Considerations include:

- Whether your wealth, subject to IHT at 40%, is below the nil-rate band (currently £325,000)
- Whether you qualify for the additional residence nil-rate band (currently £175,000)

Alternatively, as a couple, you might benefit from the transferable nil-rate band and the transferable residence nil-rate band – unused portions of a nil-rate band, as mentioned in Chapter 4 – which currently give relief up to £1 million.

Unless some of the special situations apply, as described in this chapter, you may well take the view that you should keep the arrangements for your Estate as straightforward as possible.

THE FOUR BUILDING BLOCKS OF ESTATE PLANNING

Building block 2: Lifetime giving

Having calculated your wealth, attention often turns to giving away some of that wealth in your lifetime. That giving is often to your children and grandchildren, but it can also be to other bodies such as charities, museums, galleries, government departments, local authorities and universities.

The objective of lifetime giving to children and grandchildren is to set the seven-year clock running by making potentially exempt transfers. If you survive seven years from the date of the gift, the amount given away is exempt from the charge to IHT. If you pass away after three years from making the gift, taper relief potentially applies.

Giving to charity similarly reduces the value of your Estate and the corresponding amount subject to IHT. The tax benefits of charitable giving are not limited to saving IHT at 40%; if the gift is made under Gift Aid, you will get further relief at your marginal tax rate of up to 45% for either Income Tax or Capital Gains Tax.

Lifetime giving can be in the form of absolute gifts to children and grandchildren, for example, but it can also be in the form of transferring assets into trust to benefit your children and grandchildren.

The lifetime charge to IHT at 20% may be a concern, but if the amount transferred is less than the nil-rate band, currently £325,000 per individual or £650,000 for a couple, then no IHT would be due. Also, if the assets transferred qualify for agricultural property relief or business property relief, greater amounts can be transferred without incurring an IHT liability.

Although strictly speaking not lifetime giving, the other way to reduce your wealth is to spend it – sometimes, rather technically, called de-accumulation. Any form of spending on yourself that has the effect of reducing your personal wealth will also reduce the IHT payable at the rate of 40%. You may wish to think in terms of travelling, experiencing cultural events or arranging a sumptuous family event. In any case, anything spent on yourself in effect prospectively saves IHT at 40%.

Building block 3: Structuring your Will

In the previous two building blocks, we have considered how to calculate your wealth and how to give it away in your lifetime. This, of course, all points to the inevitable – your passing – which makes properly structuring your Will the vital third block of Estate planning.

The most tax-efficient structure for the Wills of a married couple, or a couple in a civil partnership, is to create two funds:

THE FOUR BUILDING BLOCKS OF ESTATE PLANNING

1. **A discretionary trust for the surviving spouse/ civil partner, children and grandchildren:** Into this fund go assets equal to the nil-rate band (currently £325,000), together with any assets qualifying for either business property relief or agricultural property relief. These are funds and assets on which no IHT is payable on entry into the trust, and which will remain outside of the IHT Estate of the surviving spouse. They are not subject to IHT on the death of the second spouse. They will, however, be within the 6% regime, and liable to the IHT charge every ten years and on capital withdrawals, but the 6% charge payable should be minimal. Additionally, any increase in value of the assets within the fund will grow outside of the Estate of the surviving spouse, saving further IHT at 40%.

2. **A life interest trust for the surviving spouse/ civil partner:** Your children and grandchildren are also made discretionary beneficiaries of the capital of the trust fund. The terms of this fund include a wide power of appointment, which allows some or all of the trust fund to be given to any of the beneficiaries. If used to benefit the surviving spouse/civil partner, it makes no difference to the IHT payable on their Estate. If, however, used to benefit your children and grandchildren, the payment to them counts as a potentially exempt transfer by the surviving spouse/civil partner. Providing they survive seven years, it then becomes an IHT-exempt gift.

Again, this approach is the most tax-efficient structure. More importantly, it has the flexibility to carry out your wishes due to the following points:

- If only the income of the trust fund is needed by the surviving spouse/civil partner each year, then as a matter of right, they get the income of the life interest fund. Additionally, an income distribution can be made from the discretionary fund by the trustee, if needs be.

- If the income needs to be topped up for the surviving spouse/civil partner to meet expenditure for their lifestyle, the power of appointment can be used to pay some capital to the surviving spouse. This capital distribution has no IHT effect if made from the life interest fund.

- If it is perceived that the surviving spouse/civil partner is adequately provided for, the power of appointment can again be used, but this time to pay some capital to your children and grandchildren from the life interest fund. In that way, the IHT Estate of the surviving spouse/civil partner is reduced and, provided they survive seven years, this is a saving of IHT at 40% on their Estate.

In my experience, this structure works particularly well in two ways:

1. If your Estate comprises assets qualifying for 100% relief from IHT as agricultural property or business property, these essentially jump a

THE FOUR BUILDING BLOCKS OF ESTATE PLANNING

generation – from the surviving spouse/civil partner to the children and grandchildren – through the mechanism of the discretionary trust. If it is felt beneficial, these assets can stay within the discretionary trust and outside of the IHT Estate of the surviving spouse/civil partner and also that of your children and grandchildren.

2. If your Estate comprises assets subject to IHT at 40%, and it is perceived that the surviving spouse/civil partner is adequately provided for, then some of these assets can be paid to your children and grandchildren out of the life interest fund. This sets the seven-year clock running to those payments becoming IHT-exempt.

In addition, having your Estate in a trust fund means it is protected from dissipation. A trust fund also provides flexibility, meaning your Estate can be restructured, if necessary, to meet the changing needs of your family as time moves on.

What happens after the surviving spouse/civil partner dies?

Unless both spouses or civil partners die simultaneously, there will be a period where there is a surviving spouse/civil partner. There may then be a number of financial structures in existence, for example the trust fund created by the Will of the first to die or the trust funds created to hold certain assets, such as those qualifying for agricultural property relief or business property relief.

There are two viable approaches when the surviving spouse/civil partner dies:

1. **To break up the financial structures in favour of children and grandchildren:** A dynastic trust is not needed if a family's wealth is insufficient for this purpose or because the branches of the family are going in different directions or have varying needs. If the next generation is relatively young, the benefit of maintaining financial structures may be outweighed by the costs of administration. Alternatively, if your children are reaching the ends of their working lives and have no need for the funds in the financial structures, consideration could be given to 'generation jumping' – directing the funds to grandchildren to help, for example, with educational costs, house purchases or reducing their mortgages.

2. **To retain the trust funds for the next generation:** The IHT payable on the second spouse/civil partner to pass away can be used as a mechanism to get wealth into a trust fund within the 6% regime. While one generation will have borne a 40% IHT charge, future generations will not, instead having the predictable 6% regime apply to their family wealth.

Either of these approaches allows you to tailor how your private wealth is to be held and distributed once you have passed away.

Building block 4: Death benefits

This final part of Estate planning deals with those assets that have little value in your lifetime but become valuable on your death. With this in mind, consider the death benefits of your pension fund and of your life assurance policies, which provide payouts to your beneficiaries after you die.

Subject to certain conditions, rather than being paid out as a lump sum, these death benefits may be assigned to a trust fund you create in your lifetime. In this way, the value of your death benefits will pass outside of your IHT Estate, ie avoiding IHT liabilities.

The terms of this trust fund would ideally mirror those of the discretionary trust within your Will so the flexibility exists to benefit your surviving spouse and your children and grandchildren. Like your Will, this trust fund sits in the background during your lifetime, ready to come into force when you die, and in the meantime does not affect your control over your personal assets.

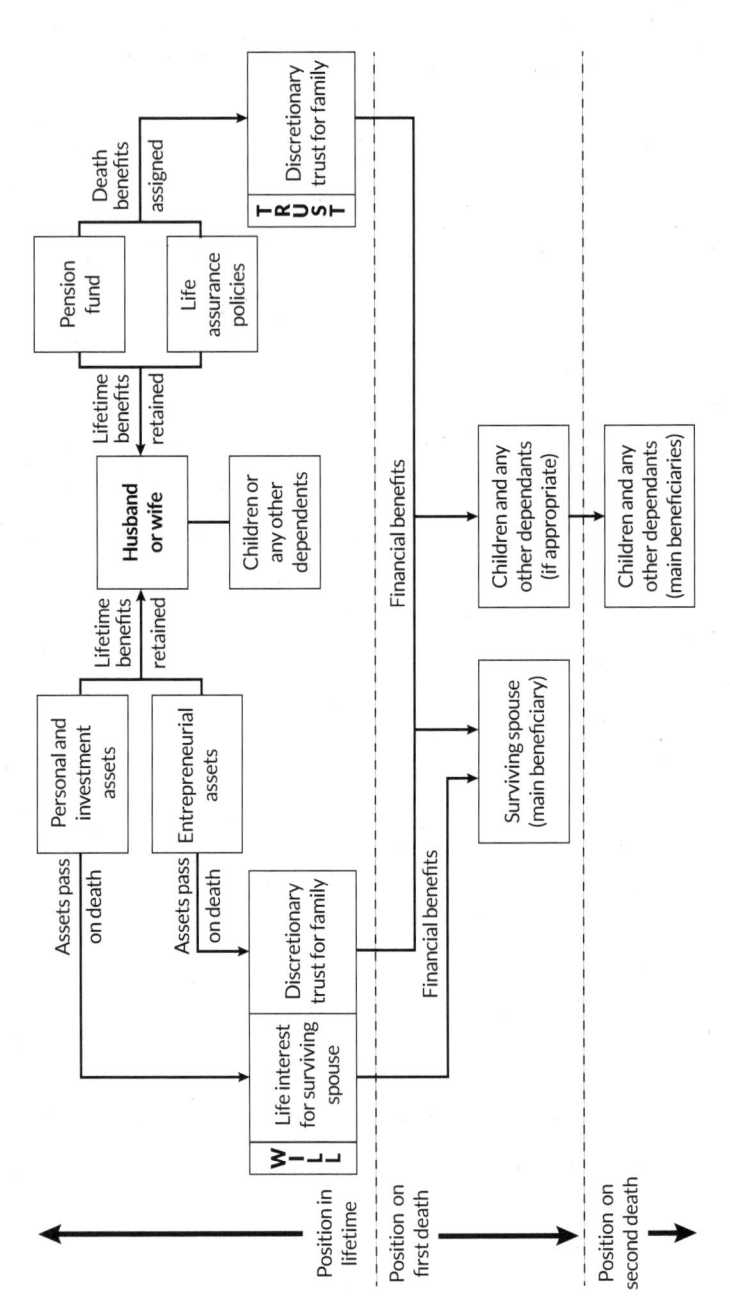

Tax-efficient Estate planning

11
Special Circumstances

In some cases, an individual's circumstances are more complex and those special circumstances will need to be taken into account on a case-by-case basis. In general, there are eight areas that often need consideration:

1. Blended families

2. Orphaned children

3. Young adults

4. International dimension

5. Persons with a disability

6. Mental incapacity

7. Unmarried parents

8. Two-year rule 'let-out'

In this chapter, I will help you identify how to deal with these special circumstances.

1. Blended families

A blended family is one where the husband and/or the wife or civil partner have a child or children from a previous relationship, where they possibly also share a child or children from their current relationship.

One of the biggest concerns in this scenario is who will inherit the money of the first spouse or civil partner to die. If their Wills have been organised in such a way that everything is left to the surviving spouse or partner (which isn't unusual or unacceptable), a problem may arise if it's left to the survivor to determine who will then inherit the Estate when they eventually die. This can lead to long and bitter family disputes; for example, if the deceased husband has two children by his first marriage and the wife has two children by her first marriage, but they have no children together. I've often seen a situation arise where the husband has, quite understandably, left his Estate to his second wife but the wife has thereafter chosen to leave everything to her own children, excluding her second husband's children. This is a cause of much dispute, often leading to litigation.

SPECIAL CIRCUMSTANCES

While the situation is often reversed, ie with the wife dying first, let's avoid confusion by continuing with the above example. It's a scenario that is almost never intended by the husband – that his children should be excluded from his inheritance. The answer may be for the husband's money to be left in trust for the benefit of his second wife, but to the extent where it's not needed, it can then pass down to the children who are listed as beneficiaries under his Will. Assuming that the intention at the outset is to benefit the children of both the husband and the wife, the trust arrangement would clearly stipulate that in the Letter of Wishes.

By ensuring that their financial affairs are properly structured during both their lifetimes, supported by a clear and unambiguous Letter of Wishes as to who should benefit once both the husband and wife have passed away, the prospect of dispute between the children from both sides of the family is significantly abated. In fact, I would argue that it would be almost impossible for any party to raise a dispute under the circumstances. Without such a plan, it's not unusual to see blended families enter into bitter and costly legal disputes.

> **CASE STUDY: Lord Templeman's Disputed Will**
>
> When Lord Templeman died, in 2014, aged ninety-four, a bitter family feud followed. His son took his stepsisters to court over his father's Will, on the grounds that he and his brother had initially been

> left most of their father's £817,000 Estate. However, Lord Templeman had also made provision for his stepdaughters to inherit a property worth £580,000. His son contested this on the basis that his father varied the terms of his Will while suffering from dementia, claiming that the Will should therefore be void.
>
> The judgement of the High Court didn't find in the son's favour, ruling that the Will was valid after finding that Lord Templeman wanted his stepdaughters by his last wife to inherit the property, because of his 'love and affection' for them. Costs of £350,000 were awarded against the son.[19]
>
> The case is an unhappy example of what can go wrong in blended families when there is ambiguity over a person's last wishes.

2. Orphaned children

Earlier I wrote about how best to select guardians for your children, and with good reason. Parents dying before their children presents a tragic set of circumstances that nobody ever wants to imagine will come true; but unfortunately, on occasions, it does.

---

19 J Ames, 'Law lord's son, Michael Templeman, left with £350,000 bill after losing battle over will', *The Times* (2020), www.thetimes.co.uk/article/law-lord-s-son-michael-templeman-left-with-350-000-bill-after-losing-battle-over-will-wbgb57rpr, accessed 27 March 2023

SPECIAL CIRCUMSTANCES

I dislike the expression 'I'm worth more dead than I am alive', but that can of course be a tragic fact of life when both parents die young, usually as the result of an accident. It's one of the main reasons (younger) parents arrange life insurance – to provide for their dependants in the event that they are indeed orphaned. If parents are young when they put this insurance in place, the life assurance companies will usually assume that their dependants won't actually need to draw on it, in the expectation that the parents will live to a good age. Consequently, the premiums are low, making it an affordable form of protection.

In the worst-case scenario, where both parents are taken, the first issue that arises is who will then look after the orphaned children, which is why it's preferable to nominate guardians, as covered in Chapter 2. The parents' wealth is then held in a series of discretionary trusts for the benefit of the children, if such arrangements are made by the parents to protect the interests of their children.

By arranging things in this way, the maximum nil-rate band of both parents is available against the personal Estate, and the value of the pension fund and the life insurance policies passes, in essence, IHT-free outside of the personal Estate. The maximum amount of money is now available to look after the newly orphaned children beyond their eighteenth birthdays and into young adulthood, in a structure that's more flexible than that of statutory trusts. Most parents, in my experience, agree that having sudden access to a large sum of money at age eighteen is inadvisable.

3. Young adults

Following that sentiment above, most parents do raise concerns that an eighteen-year-old will not yet be mature enough to inherit a large lump sum. They would rather their children first continue with their development into adulthood, to equip them with the capabilities of making good and sound decisions for themselves. As a result, most parents settle on twenty-five as the age appropriate to inherit (although I've known this to extend to thirty years and, in a more extreme example, to forty).

When considering the maturity of the offspring who are to be beneficiaries, most parents hope that their children will be settled and secure in their own lives, possibly with families of their own, by the age of thirty. A trust fund allows for these eventualities, since it provides for the money to be held for the benefit of the children until the time deemed appropriate by the parents. In the interim, the income of the trust fund could be paid to the children, and when the time is deemed right, they could then receive the capital.

Conditions of the trust are expressed in part through a Letter of Wishes and also in part through the trustees, who are given the authority to exercise their judgement having listened to requests from the children. In any event, these provisions are only necessary should the parents not live well into their old age, by which time their children will be, one hopes, mature adults in their own rights.

The risk of inheriting too much too soon

As mentioned previously, unfortunately not all parents live to see their offspring mature into responsible adults.

> **CASE STUDY: End of the high life**
>
> I was once called in to look after a trust arrangement of a high-earning stockbroker, who enjoyed the high life that came with his pay cheque. He had three children by his first marriage and was unmarried to his second partner.
>
> Sadly for him, his passing came in the form of a terminal cancer diagnosis. His Estate planning wasn't exactly well planned, and his children – all young adults – were equally used to the high life, following their father's example.
>
> With my client having left several million pounds in trust to each, the children took advantage of their generous trustees, and within ten years, the trust fund had been decimated.

4. International dimension

These days, we live more than ever in a globally connected world. Individuals who are not domiciled in a particular country are commonly known as non-doms and are typically foreign nationals who have taken up residence in the UK for a temporary purpose.

Since domicile is key to determining an individual's liability to taxation in the UK, including IHT, it attracts much controversy. This is not relevant to most people in the UK because they intend to remain here. However, for a resident foreigner in the UK, their family circumstances will most likely be different. Certainly, if they intend one day to leave the UK, domicile will matter to them in relation to IHT.

Domicile is a concept of private international law, which determines the legal jurisdiction an individual is connected to for certain purposes. A series of rules have been developed to determine an individual's domicile status. The key rules are:

- Domicile of origin is taken from the father if the person was born legitimately, ie if their parents were legally married at the time of their birth. Otherwise, domicile of origin is taken from the mother.

- Domicile of dependence for children under the age of sixteen follows the domicile of the parent on which they are dependent. If a parent's

SPECIAL CIRCUMSTANCES

domicile changes from one jurisdiction to another, the minor child's domicile follows that of the parent.

- Domicile of choice allows an individual to choose their domicile through a combination of both intention and residence. The individual needs to regard the jurisdiction as their permanent or real home, but that has to be coupled with either actual or past residence in that jurisdiction.

Sometimes described as having a strong adhesive quality, the domicile of origin is considered to be difficult to displace, or to abandon in favour of a domicile of choice. In contrast, an individual leaving the jurisdiction of their domicile of choice, with no intention of return, may well find their domicile of origin has consequently been revived in the absence of sufficient intention and presence to acquire a new domicile of choice.

If you have a domicile of origin in a jurisdiction outside of the UK, but HMRC alleges you have acquired a domicile of choice in the UK, then it's for HMRC to prove you have the domicile of choice. Conversely, if you have permanently left the UK and claim to no longer be domiciled in the UK, the burden of proof is with you.

In addition to an individual's domicile being determined under the concept of private international law, UK law has, for the purposes of IHT, introduced the concept of a deemed domicile. In the period up to 5 April 2018, an individual was deemed domiciled for IHT purposes if they had been resident in the UK for seventeen out of twenty tax years. On 6 April 2018, the rules changed, as follows:

- An individual who has been tax resident in the UK for fourteen tax years becomes deemed domiciled for IHT purposes.

- An individual previously with a domicile of origin in the UK who acquires a domicile of choice in another jurisdiction, but who then returns to the UK, will find themselves deemed domiciled in the UK from the date of their return.

- Before and after 5 April 2018, an individual who leaves the UK will be deemed domiciled in the UK for IHT purposes for the three years following their departure from the UK.

It's clear, therefore, that the concept of domicile can have a profound impact on an individual's IHT liability.

Are overseas assets liable to UK IHT?

Your domicile will determine whether your overseas assets are liable to IHT in the UK.

If you are domiciled in the UK, or if you are deemed domiciled in the UK for IHT purposes, your

SPECIAL CIRCUMSTANCES

worldwide assets will be subject to UK IHT. This is regardless of whether or not you are resident in the UK for tax purposes.

Let's look at a few examples:

- Steve left the UK to live in New Zealand but had not formed sufficient intention to stay there for the remainder of his lifetime, planning instead to move to the USA within several years. Steve's domicile of origin in the UK survived, and his asset base was split between the UK and New Zealand. When Steve died, however, his worldwide assets – both in the UK and New Zealand – were subject to UK IHT.

- Sam, an American, was seconded by his New York bank to the UK for a five-year period but died three years later. Although his wealth was held in both the UK and USA (because his domicile of origin (USA) survived), only his UK assets were subject to UK IHT.

If you are not domiciled in the UK, and not deemed domiciled in the UK for IHT purposes, your assets situated outside of the UK will not be subject to UK IHT.

What if you are internationally mobile?

Just because you are internationally mobile, moving from one country to another and never becoming tax resident in any jurisdiction, your liability to UK IHT will not be affected. If you are domiciled in the UK, or remain deemed domiciled in the UK for IHT purposes, your worldwide assets will be subject to UK IHT, even though you're not resident in the UK for tax purposes.

Are your UK assets liable to UK IHT even if you have no other connection to the UK?

Even if you are not domiciled or not deemed domiciled in the UK, if you have assets situated in the UK, they will fall within the scope of UK IHT.

Example

Gustav has lived all his life in Sweden, the same as all his relatives, other than an aunt from the UK who moved to Sweden several decades ago after marrying into Gustav's family.

The aunt owned a country home in Berkshire, which Gustav inherited when she passed away. Gustav uses the Berkshire home to attend Ascot each year but otherwise has no connection with the UK.

On Gustav's death, the Berkshire home will fall within the scope of UK IHT.

---

5. Persons with a disability

Under IHT legislation, there are essentially two ways for dealing with the situation of persons with a disability:

1. Where one of your children has a disability, the question often arises as to how your money is to be held for them when you're no longer around to look after the child. One means is the legal provision described as disabled persons' trusts or a disabled person's interest. With these trusts, current legislation removes some of the tax impacts of a discretionary trust in such a way that helps to make financial provision for a person with a disability.

2. Should both parents of a child with a disability or adult die, their money can be held in a flexible way through a discretionary trust. The trustees can therefore make such financial provision as is appropriate, ensuring that the benefits of the money are held for the child with a disability. This gives rise to another typical conversation around this special circumstance, when parents want all of their children – children with a disability included – to benefit equitably. However, often the child with a disability may have special needs, which leads the parents to expect their wealth to be skewed towards addressing that need.

> **Example**
>
> There are three children in a family. One child has a disability, and it is evident that this child will never be able to earn a living in the same way as their siblings. The parents may therefore state that they want this child to benefit to a greater extent than the other two children. A discretionary trust can make those arrangements possible. How the trustees then use the money within the trust can be determined by what is said in the Letter of Wishes. It's also important to state here that, no matter whether the child's disability gives rise to either mental or physical incapacity (or both), whatever provisions are made do not diminish that child's ability to access State support.

6. Mental incapacity

It is of course entirely possible that any one of us may fall victim to a degenerative disease such as Alzheimer's, which will then affect our mental capacity, typically in our later years.

When an individual falls prey to dementia, it's not unusual for their spouse to step up to become their primary carer, while also organising their financial affairs under a power of attorney. If the primary carer passes away, arrangements are clearly needed, not only to look after the physical needs of the spouse with dementia, but also to deal with their financial position. Once again, a trust fund provides for that special circumstance because the wealth of the deceased can be held for the benefit of the surviving spouse.

With trustees in place to administer the funds, they can then organise the appropriate financial arrangements. One other advantage of a trust fund in these circumstances is the elimination of the risk of the surviving spouse with dementia being taken advantage of financially, avoiding all manner of distress to them and their children if any inappropriate or unlawful activity is discovered.

It is essential then, for you to have a Lasting Power of Attorney to deal with both financial decisions as well as health and care decisions, in the event you lose capacity either permanently, such as in the case of a degenerative disease, or temporarily, in the case of, for example, undergoing a serious operation or recovering from an accident.

7. Unmarried parents

Of course, not all parents are married. For whatever reason, they may never get around to organising a more formal, legal arrangement such as a marriage or civil partnership, or they may simply not see the need for one. However, when one parent dies, this lack of legal agreement can cause problems with the Estate.

Under IHT law, if the deceased has left anything substantial to their partner in their Will, it unfortunately won't benefit from the spouse exemption rule, making their Estate liable to IHT. The situation may well be exacerbated if the life insurance policy and the pension policy are also paid to the executors, because then even more wealth, with an increased IHT liability, accumulates within the personal Estate.

A trust fund can help lessen this liability because the nil-rate band, and potentially also the residence nil-rate band, are available to the Estate. More importantly, the life insurance death benefit and the pension fund death benefit can pass to a discretionary trust that sits outside of the Estate. While IHT will still be due and exceed what a married couple would be liable for, this arrangement does at least reduce the amount due.

Please remember that if you've not made a Will, your partner – the co-parent of your children – will receive nothing under the law of intestacy. The use of a trust fund at least allows your partner to partially benefit from your wealth.

8. Two-year rule 'let-out'

The two-year rule simply recognises that, while you can put arrangements in place during your lifetime in the belief that they perfectly suit your needs, circumstances do change following a person's death. Therefore, the IHT legislation allows any of your

SPECIAL CIRCUMSTANCES

arrangements to be varied in the two-year period following your death, should your beneficiaries agree.

Your beneficiaries might collectively agree that your wishes aren't as fully expressed as you intended and that they would like to carry them out differently, as long as there is good reason to do so. This is based on them being able to consider the arrangements you have set out in your Will and examining whether your wishes match the outcome. If there is room to enhance those arrangements that are consistent with your intentions, IHT legislation will allow your revised wishes to be written back into the Will.

For example, where a recently deceased individual made arrangements in their Will for their business property relief assets to be included in a trust fund, it may be that the beneficiaries would prefer to own those assets personally. Those assets could be transferred to the individuals concerned while still qualifying for 100% business property relief. IHT legislation states that this elective transfer is allowable within the two-year period, and the selection will be treated as if made by the deceased and in the spirit of their original wishes.

As I've explained, death is the inconvenient truth we all must accept, which also impacts on those around us; and on occasions, special circumstances arise in many different ways. Sometimes that's because there are factors we're aware of during our lifetimes and we want to make provision for them. At other times, factors arise after we've passed away, and our heirs and successors will want to do things differently for their own reasons.

A balance must be struck between the deceased individual being able to speak from the grave and beneficiaries having the ability to make decisions for themselves. Recognising those special situations caters to both considerations.

12
The Peace Of Mind Of Having An Estate Plan

Having a plan for your Estate has the potential to give you peace of mind, as several key matters will have been addressed. For many, it is a responsible, caring and loving action, to secure your legacy and ensure that your loved ones are taken care of after you have gone.

Benefits of an Estate plan

In my experience, having an Estate plan and writing a Will allows you to address several key aspects of Estate planning. Let's look at each of them now.

1. Save time, money and stress for your loved ones.
If you die without a Will in place, your Estate falls to

be dealt with under the rules for intestacy. This can be time consuming, expensive and contentious for your loved ones, and your final wishes may not be respected.

2. Determine who will manage your Estate. When you write your Will, you have the opportunity to name your executor, or more likely, executors. These are the people who are responsible for wrapping up your Estate and should be the people you trust to carry out your wishes. If you die intestate, you will not have executors as such, but rather certain individuals related to you will be entitled to apply for what is known as a Letter of Administration. Those individuals may not necessarily be the ones you want to administer your Estate.

For example, there may be tension between the potential beneficiaries of your Estate, and if one of them were to administer your Estate to the exclusion of others it might result in a dispute between beneficiaries, which of course you would want to avoid.

3. Decide who – and who does not – get your assets and property. Testamentary freedom is an important principle in English and Welsh law. It provides people with the freedom to leave their Estate to whomever they choose in their Will, and without any legal obligation to provide for any particular family member or other individual.

You can therefore name people as beneficiaries for specific assets. You can also name beneficiaries for any property you don't list, otherwise known as the residue of your Estate.

What you might not be aware of is that you can also use a Will to help ensure that some people do not receive an equal share in your Will or anything at all. For example, you might not want someone to receive anything at all as your relationship with them has ended, such as an ex-spouse, or because you have already provided for them through lifetime giving. Or one of your children may have received additional financial support in your lifetime, and you want to equal up the division of your Estate for all of your children through your Will.

4. Choose who will look after your minor children.
The surviving parent will usually get sole custody of any children if one parent dies, but if both parents die, you can use your Will to nominate a guardian for your minor children.

Failing to nominate guardians in a Will means that the care of minor children will be decided by the courts, and in turn that could mean that someone you would not have chosen will be raising your children.

As will be appreciated, the role of guardian is an important one. It is usual for the same guardian or guardians to be appointed to look after all of your children, and it is also usual for such appointments to take effect on the death of the second parent.

5. Reduce the potential for family disputes. If you have a blended family, with children from more than one spouse or partner, that in itself is a good reason to have a Will and to set out how you would like your Estate to be inherited. In such circumstances, if you were to die intestate, some of your beneficiaries, such as an unmarried partner or stepchildren, might find themselves disinherited.

All of this can lead to friction within a family and possibly fights too, which can last a lifetime. Having a Will can reduce the potential for family disputes, as can the choice of who will be your executors.

6. Avoid unintended consequences when your circumstances change. In England and Wales, when you marry, your existing Will becomes automatically invalid, meaning your Estate will be intestate and your assets could be split up between your new spouse and your children from a previous marriage. In contrast, in Scotland, prior Wills are not invalidated by marriage meaning that your new spouse could end up with nothing.

Getting divorced does not invalidate your Will, meaning your ex-spouse could still be in line to inherit from your Estate.

It is sensible then to review your Will periodically, especially when there is a major change in your circumstances.

7. Leave a legacy and support your favourite causes. Once we are gone, most people want to leave a positive impact on the world. A great way to do this is to support the charities or causes closest to our hearts. By having a Will, you can leave a legacy to the charities or causes you wish to support and any amount given will most likely be tax efficient.

8. Provide funeral instructions. In your Will you can leave wishes for your funeral. By giving instructions, you can lessen the burden on your loved ones, and while these wishes are not binding, they can give suggestions for you to be buried or cremated, for your funeral service and its location, whether or not you would want the service to be religious, and make requests for your final resting place – is there a churchyard you wish to be buried in, for example, or a place for the ashes to be scattered?

Those instructions can extend to the hymns you might want at your funeral service, or to those you might want to give a eulogy, and indeed could also help them with details relating to your life.

9. Safeguard your digital assets. Digital accounts and purchases, such as photographs, home videos, music and video downloads and websites form part of your property. It can feel as if they have disappeared into a digital blackhole if you do not provide for access after you have passed away. You can decide if you want any information preserved or destroyed, but to do so there will need to be a record of your usernames and passwords, often best recorded in a password manager made available to your executors.

10. Provide a home for your pets. Possibly contrary to perception, the law considers a pet to be property, so you can name them as a legacy in your Will. As a legacy, you can name a beneficiary for your pet leaving them to a trusted friend or family member. In addition, you can even leave funds to provide for your pet's care.

With a pet often being a constant in many people's lives, it is no wonder that they are often described as our best friends. Being able to make provision for your pet in your Will can be a source of great comfort.

When you create a Will or update it, you can look after your loved ones and those you wish to benefit under your Will. It can provide a pathway to follow after you pass so that your financial affairs are properly wrapped up and no loose ends are left. This gives many people peace of mind, making it one of the most important reasons to have an Estate plan and to write your Will.

13
How A Letter Of Wishes Strengthens Your Estate Plan

Depending on the complexity of your financial affairs or your Estate planning, it is often the case that, in addition to a Will, there will also be a Letter of Wishes.

What, you might ask, is a Letter of Wishes?

Put simply, it is a letter to your executors and trustees to guide them in how to deal with your Estate and any trusts you have created after your death. That guidance may be on specific, sometimes difficult, matters that require discretion, and ensures they are aware of how you would approach matters if you were still alive. For this reason, a Letter of Wishes is sometimes said to allow you to speak from the grave.

There is also an important distinction between a Letter of Wishes on the one hand, and your Will on the other. A Will becomes a public document through the process of obtaining probate, but a Letter of Wishes always remains confidential to your executors and trustees. This confidentiality will enable you to feel more able to give a greater level of detail regarding your family and your financial affairs, particularly how to act in relation to particular family members or in how you want your various assets to be dealt with. Therefore, a Letter of Wishes can be written in complete privacy and may only become known after your death. Alternatively, it may be a letter you wish to openly discuss with your executors and trustees, as this may provide greater clarity around how they will act after you have passed away.

The usual contents of a Letter of Wishes are wide ranging and below I give examples of matters that are often included. One area to be careful about is ensuring that your Letter of Wishes does not include anything that contradicts your Will. But once that point is addressed, a Letter of Wishes often speaks on:

- Instructions on who to notify of your death, or in some cases, who not to tell
- Your funeral instructions (if they are not in your Will)
- Details of how your personal possessions are to be distributed (usually given in a separate Letter of Wishes for what are known as your chattels)

HOW A LETTER OF WISHES STRENGTHENS YOUR ESTATE PLAN

- Guidance on how you would like any property or money you leave to be managed
- In relation to any trusts, details relating to the main beneficiaries and your wishes about when to make payments of either capital or income to them, and the intended longevity of the trust
- Also in relation to any trusts, whether the trustees should generation jump by passing assets down a generation, for example bypassing your children in favour of your grandchildren
- If you have minor children, advice to your guardians on how your children should be raised, their education and where they live and the financial provision available to them until they become adults
- If you leave minor children or young adults, the age at which they might be considered sufficiently financially responsible to receive large sums of capital
- In the event you have reduced or excluded a legacy to someone who might expect to inherit from your Estate, an explanation as to why, if you think your decision might be controversial or may be challenged at a later date

There are few formalities relating to a Letter of Wishes. First, it does not have to be formally drawn up or witnessed. Indeed, it would be better if it was not witnessed, as this may imply it is an addition to or replacement of your existing Will, or that it has become a Codicil to your Will. Second, a Letter of Wishes can be updated any time you wish, which, in contrast to your Will, is either added to with a Codicil or a new Will is itself drawn up. This flexibility, with the confidentiality, often makes a Letter of Wishes an invaluable document to help with your Estate planning.

It is usual for a Letter of Wishes to be drawn up at the same time as your Will. It is important that you do not forget, contradict or duplicate anything in your Will, as you would not want your wishes to be disregarded. It is worth remembering the Letter of Wishes is there to support the clear instructions in your Will.

Although I suggest you draw up the Letter of Wishes at the same time as your Will, you can of course update your Letter of Wishes at any time as your circumstances or intentions change.

If it is a good idea to review your Will every five years, then it is a good idea to review your Letter of Wishes every year. Finally, a good place to store your Letter of Wishes is with your Will.

I hope you will understand the importance I place on a Letter of Wishes, and how a well-drafted Letter of Wishes can only strengthen your Estate plan and your Will.

Conclusion

This book has captured the key processes that I guide my clients through when making arrangements for their Wills. It shows that there are numerous opportunities for you to reduce your IHT liabilities, and that there are a variety of ways to approach succession planning and passing on a family business.

Each individual's circumstances are unique, and sometimes the path ahead may not always seem clear. However, I trust that this book has:

- Helped you consider options you'd never imagined were possible and, as a result, allayed some of your concerns about who will get your money when you die

- Offered you a clear understanding of how the UK IHT system works and whether you face an IHT liability, and if so, the measures you can take to reduce that liability

If you've been wondering how and when to approach matters of succession planning for your business, then you'll consider seeking impartial and critical advice before you make any provisions for your family to take over its running, when that might not be the best option for all involved.

If there are special circumstances within your family that on the surface seem problematic, I hope this book will have given you some peace of mind in the knowledge that there are always efficient and advantageous ways to deal with most situations.

The four building blocks and the final diagram in Part Three offer a clearly structured framework, which you can employ in your considerations around IHT. Once you've identified the options that best suit your family's interests, implementing the plan will then sit in the background until it's needed.

Remember, IHT is a voluntary tax because you can control how much of your Estate pays or retains its wealth. The outcome of your considerations will be that you'll know your wealth is inherited in a way that reflects your wishes. You will have been able to use the available opportunities that allow you to reorganise

CONCLUSION

your financial affairs and reduce the impact of taxation. It will be then your intended beneficiaries that get to keep more of your money when you die.

I wish you the very best in considering the one singularly important issue of making a Will so that, when confronting the inconvenient truth that one day we must all die, at least you then will be able to do so having left behind arrangements to ensure your final life wishes are carried out.

Acknowledgements

Every author says, 'I couldn't have written this book without so and so,' and that is always true.

First, a big thank you to my clients, with whom it has been a privilege to work and who have shaped my experiences beyond my wildest dreams.

Then to the team at Ritchie Phillips LLP. They have read the manuscript – often more than once – and have given willingly in their encouragement and constructive criticism as this book emerged towards publication. Included in this team is Lucy Pitts, who has been with me from the start, in planning and writing this book and getting it finished.

Thank you to those who reviewed this book before publication, especially Laura Dadswell, who provided the foreword, and Matthew Hutton (author of *Your Last Gift: Getting your affairs in order*), who took it upon himself to act as a much-welcomed critic of the technical aspects of this book.

Thanks to Rethink Press and Dent Global, who have helped create something beyond my expectations, which I hope will make a positive impact in an underserved area of society, allowing individuals to make meaningful decisions in respect of their Estate planning.

Finally, thank you to my wife, Caroline, and son, Matthew, who have been a greatly valued constant as this book has come to fruition.

The Author

Stuart has over thirty years' experience of high-net-worth private client taxation, including inheritance and succession planning.

He is a fellow of the Institute of Chartered Accountants in England and Wales (ICAEW) and a member of the Chartered Institute of Taxation. He is also chair of the ICAEW Tax Faculty Private Client Committee.

Stuart trained and studied while working for Rawlinson & Hunter, one of the leading private client accountancy firms in London. Once a qualified chartered accountant and chartered tax advisor, he began working in private client taxation, as well as being exposed to Inheritance Tax and the giving of succession advice, working with clients of the highest profile and with complex high-value entities.

After six years with Rawlinson & Hunter, he took up the position of manager at the relatively small private client accountancy firm Dixon Wilson, where he progressed to become a partner.

In 2003, he founded his own accountancy firm Ritchie Phillips LLP, which specialises in private client taxation.

Stuart is married to Caroline. They are blessed with a son, Matthew, and their home is currently dominated by their two dogs, Jago and Jowan. When not working, Stuart enjoys sport, playing cricket, golf and real tennis. He also enjoys culinary delights, all the more so if they can be combined with the arts.

🌐 https://ritchiephillips.co.uk